THE CONFESSIONS
OF A PUZZLED PARSON

THE CONFESSIONS
OF A PUZZLED PARSON

AND OTHER PLEAS FOR REALITY

BY
CHARLES FISKE
BISHOP OF CENTRAL NEW YORK

BR
85
.F54

ESSAY INDEX

Essay Index Reprint Series

97330

BOOKS FOR LIBRARIES PRESS
FREEPORT, NEW YORK

First Published 1928
Reprinted 1968

LIBRARY OF CONGRESS CATALOG CARD NUMBER:
68-54345

PRINTED IN THE UNITED STATES OF AMERICA

FOREWORD

OF course I am not as puzzled or penitent as I describe myself. The thoughts about the pernicious activity of paid uplifters to which expression is given in two of these papers are not of recent date; they ceased to be doubts long ago; even in prewar days, long before the present era of persistent propaganda, they became convictions. I have seen no reason, during these years, to change my mind.

Nor have I discovered any argument which would bring about my conversion in the matter of the political activities of American churches. It has been an encouragement to find that thousands of laymen agree so heartily with some of these pronouncements that they have been moved to unbosom themselves in most enthusiastic epistolary confessions. It has been of interest, at the same time, to discover that those who disagree most violently usually write anonymously, and invariably in language that is ungrammatical as well as lurid. I doubt whether any of them would consider me penitent were they to supply names and addresses and allow me to reply.

Certain friendly commentators who have read

the essays declare that not only do they show no signs of bewilderment, but that the writer is evidently no more penitent than puzzled. They have called me a sapient and satirical sophisticate, have described me as an ebullient etymologist, have suggested that the essays are, in spots, echinulate, though acknowledging that the author could not be charged with echolalia. Once I was actually accused of being the *enfant terrible* of the episcopate, because I so freely examined the failings of bishops and clergy. Some correspondents apparently have mental images of me which lead them to think that I am a violent and aggressive person, whereas I am truly the mildest-mannered ecclesiastic that ever cut a throat.

The essays in this volume deal with a variety of subjects, and in a variety of ways. They may seem, therefore, somewhat disconnected. The careful reader will find in them, however, very definite and decided beliefs, repeated and emphasized in connection with widely different subjects, but making a thread of conviction which ties the whole together. Two of the chapters, I fear, read a bit like sermons. They are not preachments, but are the substance of addresses given at religious conventions. They are included in the volume, though so different in tone and style, because they deal with real convictions, the holding of which makes me critical of certain tendencies of American re-

ligionists. I would not wish to be judged by the
critical tone of the first essays, save as set over
against the serious thought of these later addresses
of a more constructive character.

The essays are all pleas for reality in religion,
for honest inquiry into the problems, ethical or
social, economic or political, with which religion
may be concerned. They are impatient of "pussy-
footing." They express root convictions with which
others may disagree—as they are free to do, if
they will allow me the same privilege as to their
beliefs, and join in an effort to help both sides to
"disagree agreeably."

Acknowledgment is made to *Scribner's Maga-
zine, Harper's, The Atlantic Monthly, Forum,
The American Mercury,* and to the Macmillan
Company, for permission to reprint from articles
published by them.

CONTENTS

A PENITENT AND PUZZLED PARSON

A PENITENT AND PUZZLED PARSON

I

I MAY describe myself as a social reformer who has at last undertaken the task of reforming himself. If not yet wholly reformed, I am at least penitent. For a long time I have been undergoing the pains of conversion, wrestling in quiet over many things that puzzle the mind and torture the spirit. Now and then I have spoken to relieve my soul, but in the main I have been thinking—or trying to think.

The ministers of America are partially responsible for my present disquiet. They have made me see myself as others see *them*. And the advocates of various social movements are also partly responsible for my timid approach to the mourner's bench. As one sometimes hears the ticking of the clock, even amid the din of roaring machinery, so the rattling of reform drums and the blowing of welfare trumpets, as they blare forth insistently, have but made clear to the ear the sound of a still, small voice ringing above the battle-cry of executive secretaries and minor officers of the social-welfare hosts. It may be that some rude persons with nothing but ribald jeers for men of the cloth have

3

been instrumental, to some degree, in producing the pains of penitence. Underneath the brazen notes of their assaults (which good men denounce as coming from Satan's seat) there are undertones of truth to which one finds oneself uncomfortably tempted to listen. The sight of the gorgeous office-building near the Capitol in Washington, where busy secretaries further the cause of public morals, has also furthered my conversion—as is eminently proper, even though the conversion has been shunted to the wrong switch. The discovery that there are over 150 central agencies having offices in Washington, and as many more in New York, representing all sorts of interests, fads, and fancies, has reacted upon my evangelical fervor and mixed me in mind. I am like the young man who, when he heard that his best girl was a somnambulist, declared that he was sick of denominational disputes, and though he was brought up a Baptist would willingly go to her church.

I am not only penitent, I am puzzled. In planning a future programme, I put it forth tentatively. Truth to say, the path is just appearing, and it is difficult to know where it may lead. For a time we haven't seen the woods because of the trees. As a puzzled penitent I may possibly see things more clearly by throwing some experiences upon the screen. This is a sad mixing of metaphor, but emotional strain is careless of correct rhetoric.

Suppose we change the figure again: some of us have been running so hard in the reform race that our breath is gone. Other eager advocates of various panaceas for the betterment of society, business, industry, the municipality, the church, and national and international relations, have been flitting from flower to flower like bees who gather honey every day—only they hardly hover over any one flower long enough to gather much honey.

An expert spiritual diagnostician would probably declare that my grave state of health is due to the fact that I have been too frequently exposed to the contagion of executive secretaries. They range over a multitude of activities—civic, humanitarian, ecclesiastical, and political. They multiply until they have become, like the sands which are on the seashore, innumerable. If some one had kept a catalogue of all the reforms which have been urged upon my consideration in the past fifteen years, the list would look so formidable that the sympathies of the most violent of uplifters might, for a moment, be aroused in behalf of the victim of their combined assaults.

Ah, how many June-bugs of reform I have allowed myself to chase! It is painful to tell about them, because the enumeration carries us back into so distant a past that it will reveal to friends the age of their penitent parson, and, of course, I don't want them to think of me merely as a nice old gentleman who for many decades has been too gently kind to discourage the progress of the professional uplifter. Yet, if some of us could only hit the sawdust trail, what a confession would pour from our lips as we told of the flittings into pastures new, to which we have been led by the Chief Butterflies. Back we go to the days when we were sure that votes for women would reform politics; still further back, to the beginnings of the prohibition movement, which has since grown into an octopus with so firm a hold that it makes the reform of politics more difficult than in the era of the saloon. How vivid are the days when we engaged in a campaign for eugenic marriage, only to find some popular clergyman taking us seriously, and in endeavoring to follow our advice with his "society congregation," passing many a sleepless night before all was forgiven and forgotten! How long ago it seems, and how mild was the sensation it created, looking back now, in these days of "birth control"!

And what grand times those were when now and then we welcomed a modern John the Baptist in the person of some Christian Socialist! He was a Daniel, but a second Daniel come to judgment, as we discovered later on, when another brother came into our midst combating his theories, and again the call went out to hold up the hands of the leader who played the Moses to his

Aaronic rôle. To think that one is old enough to
remember those first parlor Socialists, and to have
such vivid recollections of what happened when
the proletariat discovered and used the pink pellets of the *intelligentsia* of that dim and distant
day; and yet how pale by comparison with the
reign of clever young men and women of to-day
who engage in literary log-rolling to help the public to discover how wonderful they all are, each
radical unveiling the brilliancy of the other to our
dazzled eyes.

And then to think that one is old enough to
remember the first Community Christmas-tree,
and how it had hardly been brought down ere its
place was taken by the pennant-poles of a dozen
new social movements. To particularize still further: one remembers the year when we were all
in hysterics over the red-light district, and were
told of rescued maidens who turned out to be
models of womanly virtue. There was another year
when we were agitated over prison reform—sadly
needed, of course, but (after we had taken hold
of it) trailed in a parade of mushy sentimentality
that would have been amusing had it not been so
pathetically tragic in its consequences. Still another year found us pushing the work of the Con-
sumers' League, only to find that the progressive
head of it had led us on to the reform of the ship-
ping laws. Indeed, we usually moved on toward

new endeavors before awaking to the discovery
that it is not enough to put laws on the statute-
books, and quite as important to educate the public conscience after legislation has been passed as
before. Having secured possession of the pen that
signed an act, we usually, in those days, left the
law to its fate.

What a panorama the years were, after that, for
the serious-minded: from men and religion to
men and missions; thence to Billy Sunday and
the sawdust trail; from anti-vivisection to an anti-
noise crusade; from sex hygiene and sex education in the public schools to "damaged goods" and
the reform of the movies; from Christian unity
to the dove of international peace; and then, so
soon, to war propaganda, in which (praise be!)
I can pride myself that I kept my feet on the
ground and refused to soar into the blue empyrean, though I did endeavor to do the real work
one felt a real spiritual crisis called for.

Not that one could always be so safe—we
"joined" again and again. The League of Nations
agitation, the plans of the American Peace Society, and the Peace League of the World, the agitation for the defeat of the Turkish treaty, the
dispute over the war debts—these were all large
problems on which we felt quite competent to
pass, while in the more limited sphere of domestic reform we were at the mercy of retired preach-

ers, unsuccessful evangelists, ambitious press
agents and newspaper men out of a job, who en-
listed our efforts in many new movements out
of which they were making a fair living. There
was even an organization of municipal employees
engaged in agitating for a new form of city man-
agement, and so creating new jobs and opening
up larger fields of activity to which they themselves could be promoted. There were associations
for and against prohibition; Americanization organizations loomed up at every crossroad; business conventions mingled religious fervor with
high-power salesmanship; propagandist orders
grew apace; we were trained in publicity methods; our agents crowded the legislative lobbies.
Executive secretaries descended upon us daily,
and every week a new organization was born with
new offices opened and a new secretary function-
ing. Only a few months ago there came an invitation to become a director of the National Committee for the Education of Women in Financial
Matters and the Protection of Her Money. It
made the worm turn. I decided to decline the invitation and devote my spare time to organizing
a Society for the Protection of Trustful Parsons
and their Defense Against the Paid Uplifter.

So there came for me the day of awakening.
The demands upon time and energy became so
great that I rebelled.

II

Is all this the real work of the ministry? Or have we been neglecting work distinctly our own to engage in that which is as distinctly in the province of others? Not, of course, that we should preach to others while we ourselves were "on refreshment" and idle—if not active, we could be interested—but are we not spreading our efforts too thin? Can one small brain contain all the expert knowledge necessary to settle all the affairs of the universe? Conceivably, may not others know far more than we of the complicated problems at issue in such matters as the minimum wage and child labor and women in industry? Was not the defeat of the Child Labor Amendment a warning against overmuch meddling? Could we not have trusted the Department of State in some delicate matters about which we had been blatantly free with advice? And should we not each stick to *one* thing and let other people do the thing they choose, without imagining that the momentary object of our own enthusiasm is the only cause that must obtrude upon the public eye? Is not overlegislation a curse? Are not some of the reform and welfare proposals half-baked theories? Would it not be well to cultivate a sense of humor? Or, at least, a sense of proportion? Are we ministers making ourselves a general nuisance?

I began to be penitent for past activity; over-

activity; excessive attendance upon the affairs
of the city, the State, the nation, the poor, the
slums, the working men, the women and children, the social democracy. Others, also, began to
feel that perhaps it might be well occasionally to
let people manage their own affairs and regulate
their own morals. Of course there were friends
to tell us that reform really was the business of
a clergyman, that the minister must be a man of
affairs, that he ought not to rest content with
preaching general moral principles and never specifically applying them. I admit that this ra'her
put me on the horns of a dilemma, and I began to
have fears as to where I might fall when tossed.
Can any one help me to solve the difficulty? Because, wherever I fall, I know it will hurt.

When I began making a few feeble protests—
voicing doubts as to the Eighteenth Amendment;
hinting that there were religious movements to-
day that made me long to disguise myself in non-
clerical clothes—some of the brethren called me a
quitter. They said that I was piping for peace
while the war-steeds were sniffing the battle from
afar. The only peace in which a minister should
be interested was not surcease from vocal agitation, but abstention from armed conflict, and
really he couldn't do his best work there unless
he had received a visit from the paid agent of the
American Union Against Militarism.

Well, I knew there was a flaw in their argument, but I was puzzled; just as I knew there was something wrong in our welfare programme, but could not be certain what it was or where. Like the man who sat on the cat, I had my suspicions—you remember he could not see the cat, but *somehow he felt that it was there!* What was wrong? Somewhere we had made a mistake, but just where? and when? and how?

III

A witty Frenchman has declared that "all generalizations are wrong, especially this one." Therefore, there will be much in the present generalization about which the readers will utterly disagree with the writer—and probably with each other. Indeed, the writer will possibly be at disagreement with many of his own statements; for it will be necessary, in order to make his point clear, to generalize on broad lines and paint the picture in high coloring. With this patent attempt at disarming harsh criticism, let us proceed to our protests, confident that many an aggrieved victim will sing an "Amen" to each of the statements made.

First, I have come to the conclusion once voiced by an inmate of one of our State hospitals for the insane, who declared that he knew exactly what is wrong with the world and how to remedy it. "The thing that is wrong with the world," he said, "is that there is entirely too much talking. They put me here because I wanted to kill off some of the public orators and after-dinner speakers."

There are now so many conventions, conferences, discussion groups, commissions, and uplift gatherings of every sort, that any one of us may have a perfectly grand time travelling about and attending conferences designed to show what should be done, and foregathering with those who are so busy learning what to do that they have little time to do what awaits their zeal and knowledge. In my own church I find it expected of me that I shall attend over fifty different ecclesiastical gatherings each year, and the number could easily be increased were it not for perpetual vigilance on my part. Indeed, these but make up the normal list in the actual sphere of duty; add the various activities outside the church, and the number is at once doubled. And what do the gatherings accomplish? I remember hearing an enthusiastic attendant at one of them say, "What a wonderful convention—really revolutionary in its attitude toward the problems presented"; whereupon a cynic sniffed and snorted: "Revolutionary? No; Resolutionary!"

Second, there come more than occasional doubts as to the character of much of our welfare work. It has been commercialized and professionalized to such an extent that a special kind of appeal is now made for its support—an appeal to pride of patronage from wealth, and often to fears of radicalism as well—and one begins also to feel that much of the work is an excuse for the difficulty of real thought and conviction.

The average American business man has been encouraged to believe himself religious if he sings long and loud about the duty of service, and insists that, unlike virtue which is its own reward, service (with a large S) brings monetary returns of a real material worth. America has become almost hopelessly enamoured of a religion that is little more than a sanctified commercialism; it is hard in this day and this land to differentiate between religious aspiration and business prosperity. Our conception of God is that he is a sort of Magnified Rotarian. Sometimes, indeed, one wonders whether the social movement and the uplift in general have not become, among Protestants, a substitute for devotion; worse than that, a substitute for real religion. Efficiency has become the greatest of Christian virtues. I hope I may be forgiven a note of exaggeration that is necessary to make my meaning clear when I say that Protestantism, in America, seems to be degenerating into a sort of Babsonian cult, which cannot distinguish between what is offered to God and what is accomplished for the glory of America and the furtherance of business enterprise.

Third, these doubts as to the character and efficiency of welfare work arise from a consideration of the type of people engaged in it. These are, for the most part, secretaries, assistant secretaries, and paid publicity men, all serving at comfortable salaries. The proportion of publicity to actual accomplishment is appalling in volume. We have caught the spirit of the trade associations; only with them there is usually a definite bill to be forced through the legislature, while the welfare host is more vague in its aspirations. When captains of industry, kings of commerce, and vociferous reformers unite, the story is different—then, indeed, things happen. Doubtless many philanthropists whose purses are opened to the demands of the "uplifters" half consciously understand the possibilities of such combination; but most of them merely get a certain satisfaction from the feeling that they are "doing good," and only an expert could tell how much of their money goes into office rent, stenographic labor, propaganda, travel, conference and convention appropriations, and the salaries of those who function as executives.

Charity is not only professionalized, it is commercialized. Ministers who weary of the humdrum round of parish work make up a considerable body of the employed. Only an expert statistician could estimate how many of them have trailed through Russia and Europe to the Near East. Young women who are uncertain of other employment seem to find a ready outlet for their enthusiasms and a comfortable living in the cause of social betterment. Youthful doctrinaires who are out of a job labor over poorly digested programmes of reform. All endeavor to "magnify their office," and brains are busily occupied in formulating plans, projects, and programmes for churches and associations, until those who are supposed to put these programmes into practical operation are driven near to madness. So many things are proposed that little is actually accomplished; overlapping in work becomes the rule rather than the exception; overhead expense increases by leaps and bounds; exorbitant financial demands lead to numerous drives; these campaigns furnish employment to hundreds of other well-paid experts; eager volunteers catch the lure of professionalism and industriously develop new openings, and it has come to a pass where it is hardly possible to get any work done, unless some one is paid to tell us how to do it, some one else paid to raise the necessary funds, and others paid to do it for us.

And, fourth, when they are paid, they do it badly. If the real accomplishments of the various social agencies were closely examined, it would be discovered that common sense is distressingly absent in executive officers. Occasionally the professional worker is case-hardened; more often, the young women who serve in these various missions of help are sentimental in the extreme, actually engaged in propagating the largest of modern organizations, the Great Society of the Outstretched Hand. There are women engaged in the work of reclaiming their wayward sisters who sentimentally rush them into new temptations. There are church orphanages whose one idea of welfare work is to baptize babies by the dozen. There are children's aid societies whose secretaries were appointed because somebody on the board had an unsuccessful minister he wanted to "place." There are probation officers whose positions were secured by social or political pulls. Everywhere are evidences that anybody who cannot make a living, or secure a recognized position in other ways, looks to welfare work as an easy way of moving ahead socially and drawing a fair salary allowance at the same time. For the social worker sometimes meets "the best people," and her position gives her a feeling of importance that is soul-soothing in the highest degree.

Perhaps the evil might be checked if the title of executive secretary could be abolished. A young woman with six months' experience in a larger organization is made executive secretary in a smaller city, and at once she must have elaborate offices, stenographers, an automobile, paid helpers and reams of stationery, even before she has discovered what work there is to do. Check the megalocephalic growth that begins with the conferring of a high-sounding title, and perhaps we shall save some of the young women from their own explosive tendencies. As for the young men—what can check their telegrams, letters, appeals, exhortations, legislative activities, expert advising, varied impertinences, and annual drives and campaigns, only the dim future may reveal.

IV

Those of us who had anything to do with war work during the Great Upheaval, whether at home in the camps or on the other side, will remember the supreme contempt for the Y.M.C.A. which the dough-boy expressed in language of a varied and picturesque and racy richness. We have had many explanations of the dislike the "Y" encountered, all of them more or less true; but many of us were convinced that the chief cause of its unpopularity lay in the fact that the "Y" was the quintessence of the uplift. It was the commonest and worst manifestation of the sort of moral activity whose victims were always peculiarly and especially resentful. In the breasts of 100-per-cent Americans was engendered a yearning for sweetness and light; a passion for service. Everybody was anxious to improve his neighbor; the road to heaven was a road of high moral endeavor in making some one else good. There was the army right at hand to practise on, and in rushed the third-rate preachers, the vocational trainers, the circulating librarians, the "Y" men (some of whom might have done military duty), the vice crusaders, the motherly women, girl entertainers seeking a thrill, and moral reformers of every shade of eccentricity.

An army officer recently expressed publicly his resentment of the fact that the pious work begun in war-time under the inspiring leadership of the college professor who acted as third or fourth assistant secretary of war is still continued in the effort of a Kiwanian-minded adjutant-general to train on lines of good citizenship the men who remain in the army. He paints a fascinating picture of the effect of a poem by the late Franklin K. Lane on the gay vagabond who leads the chorus at the end of a long hike. He sings another poem than Mr. Lane's: "You'll never get rich, you'll die in the ditch, you're in the army now." Here, for example, is the last question in the final chapter of the "Studies in Citizenship" arranged by the official army uplifter: "What is democracy? Can it make all people healthy, wealthy, and wise? What can a democracy do? When can it do it? Who will do it? Why?" The indignant officer declares that he will omit these questions when he has occasion to give instruction in the course. He is afraid some one will ask him the answers. And then he adds, with possibly pardonable profanity: "Damn the uplift and the uplifters."

I am convinced that this army officer but expresses, in rude and unpolished language, the vaguer feelings of tens of thousands—hundreds of thousands—of persons, in and out of the churches, who find themselves increasingly out of sympathy, not merely with the methods of the Anti-Saloon League, the Lord's Day Alliance, and the Methodist Board of Temperance, Prohibition, and Public Morals, but with welfare organizations in general; sometimes, because these have been contaminated by the methods of the more conspicuous organizations; more often, because there is a growing impatience of smugness in religion, of the over-regulation of morals, of the pharisaical combination of business and religion, or of philanthropy and fear of radicalism, of overprofessionalism in public service of any sort, social, religious, charitable, or political reform.

Add to this the thought of numerous organizations for propaganda, with the flood of flimsy which they pour upon the news-editor's desk, and it is not surprising to find that we cannot read the daily paper with our old-time conviction that whatever we see in print must be true. A larger number of people than most of us imagine have reached the point where they are suspicious of everything

they read and are ready to discount more than
half that the newspapers print. They know how
much of it is the propagandist output of various
societies whose paid secretaries work for associations with ready access to the moneyed interests,
and have well-filled chests with which to produce
a semblance of public opinion. The result is that
they become equally suspicious of almost all moral
movements organized along modern lines. It is
unfortunate, but it is true, that they are also becoming resentful of much welfare work. Americanization sometimes seems to them a subtle Protestant propaganda. Community charity appears
as an easy way for many otherwise inactive persons to make a living. Even religious work of a
distinctive character is tinged with suspicions as
to its real motives and the sincerity of the workers.
It may grieve some who are giving of their very
best in support of a cause in which they are deeply
interested, but it is a condition that ought to be
faced. Part of the duty of facing it will be the call
to men and women whose money now supports
paid workers. That call will be a searching question: Can you not give of yourself as well as of
your money? If you are honestly concerned about
human betterment, can you any longer turn the
whole task over to a salaried employee to do in your
stead? If you really believe in the thing you are
paying for, may not your amateur effort accomplish more than the professional work of the per-

son who does what you are not now willing to do? And are you quite sure—you men and women whose purses are opened to the call of many causes —are you quite sure that, actually, you are giving to help a cause, or forward a movement, or cure a social evil, and not "chipping in" with those who are "keeping the lid down"?

V

Having said all this, I am quite aware of the natural and logical reply that will be on the tongue of every one who disagrees with me. Are not the clergy themselves paid uplifters? Am I not putting myself and my brethren out of business?

Bless your soul, that is the very thing that irritates and annoys me; because, in plain fact, there is so little similarity between the life of a clergyman who engages in spiritual service on a salary that would starve a sparrow and his brother minister who has joined the uplift and lives in the limelight, delivering seven lectures seventy times seven times each, and being paid more for his service than he could ever possibly hope to earn by going to work.

Moreover, I conceive of the ministry as something more than glorified "Y" work. The minister, to my old-fashioned mind is a man used by God

to reveal God's truth, speaking as God's representative and as the authorized teacher of a church
which holds the deposit of faith, not uttering his
own passing fancies and furthering his own fads,
nor passionately championing the latest cause and
setting forth the newest moral issue, but declaring
the mind of the church as an *ecclesia docens*. Especially do I conceive of the minister as the human
instrument for conveying divine grace in the sacraments which he celebrates. What grieves my soul
is the fact that I am more likely to be regarded as
a super Y.M.C.A. secretary—which is an excellent
office for those who like it. It happens to be about
the last occupation I would choose in this world
or care to be held responsible for in the next, but
this is a personal prejudice for which I apologize
and which limitations of space make it impossible
for me to explain and defend.

In welfare work, so far as it concerns religious
activities, we may note a threefold classification.
There are the Roman Catholics, who know exactly
where they stand and what they want to do and
how. There are those who for a better name may
be called Humanitarians, who just as definitely
believe in work separated from religion, and from
any divine compulsion. Finally, there are the Protestants, who once had very definite convictions,
and are now somewhat at sea; here and there
substituting humanitarianism for worship, else-

where clinging to the individualistic conception of religion, always lacking any corporate idea of Christianity either in faith or practice. As an impertinent bit of propaganda I may remark that the conception of my own church I believe to be theoretically most sane, combining what is best in Catholicism with the emphasis Protestantism has placed upon the second commandment of the new law. In practice, however, the average Episcopal clergyman is apt either to move enthusiastically toward the Catholic ideal or, on the other hand, to become enamoured of the Protestant belief that the minister is primarily a welfare leader and only secondarily a duly commissioned priest and pastor. And, of course, with this latter conception, he is an easy mark for every new "movement," wherever it may originate and whithersoever it may be moving.

Once more: I know that from every side will rise a Babel of voices declaring that Christianity is a social gospel, not merely a gospel of individual salvation; that it is a leaven to leaven the whole lump; that it has to do with industrial and economic ethics, with community and national life, with international relations.

Of course. Nobody but a fool could fail to see it. But many who are not fools fail to see the difference between holding up a moral ideal and laying down the particular method by which it may be attained. The church supplies a spiritual dynamic.

Jesus Christ brought into life a new spirit which, if it be taken seriously and honestly, will change the world. But he passed no laws, inaugurated no new industrial organization, framed no social platform, set forth no political panaceas. Moral issues may sometimes be so plain that the church can express its corporate mind on' the subject, but for the most part the methods by which right moral action shall be taken are open to grave differences of opinion. One may believe that the Volstead Act embodies the ethical judgment of America; another may believe that there is little force of public opinion behind it. One man may believe that the use of fermented drink is always a sin; another may believe that at the most a Christian should be called upon to practise total abstinence only on the basis of the Pauline injunction, lest he cause his weaker brother to offend. Indeed, I see no reason to condemn unheard the man who feels that the present attitude toward temperance is puritanically intemperate, and that he should use wine without abusing it. All may be equally sincere Christians.

When we come to other matters of social legislation involving economic principles and dealing with commercial or industrial conditions, the room for disagreement is even larger. What right have I to impugn the honesty or denounce the morals of a man who may not spring upon the band-wagon when the reformers tune up about the minimum wage, the shortened day's work, old-age pensions, the Shepherd-Towner method of paying for pre-natal care, or a dozen other hastily prepared pro-grammes of social legislation?

It is, therefore, with the expectation of hearing a prolonged sevenfold Amen from the suffering laity that I voice a prayer for the church that it may escape the perils of the professional uplift, and learn that there is a way we may do our proper work and yet set forth a social gospel.

And it is in the sure and certain conviction that the evils of paid propaganda are closely allied with the over-organization of paid welfare work, that I confidently expect, along with fresh criticism, an equally warm and ready sympathy in the confes-sion so publicly made and the puzzled question-ings of my own heart so penitently set down. They are set down in the vague desire that they may be constructively answered; in the expecta-tion, however, that they may stir up secretarial indignation; in an irredeemable optimism which still hopes that we may learn to discriminate be-tween propaganda and fact; in steadfast hope that social-service enthusiasts may some day learn to do a bit more work and a little less travelling, lecturing, and listening. At any rate, I am sure that many others are as weary as myself of the pernicious activity of the paid uplifter.

BRINGING IN THE MILLENNIUM

BRINGING IN THE MILLENNIUM

I

REBELS in revolt against 100-per-cent American-
ism and the smug piety which is one of its chief
ingredients may resent admitting to the fold a
wearer of purple-and-fine-linen vestments. And
what may not happen to the ecclesiastic who is
discovered in the company of these wild disturbers
of our placid peace? He has the courage to rush
into the danger zone only because he knows that
there are many whose hearts will beat in sympathy
with his mild and hesitating protests.

Even a conservative, cautious ecclesiastic may
feel bound in honor to record his misgivings—
which many another parson frequently shares.
He sees in all churches hundreds of his brethren
"seeking refuge from the difficulties of thought in
the opportunities for action." He sees scores of
his friends resigning an inspirational ministry to
accept ecclesiastical positions as field secretaries
or swivel-chair reformers. He sees churches abandoned to the unrestrained energy of social uplifters who are experts in politics of every type,
from the common garden variety upward. He sees
the slow and patient process of reforming the world
through reforming individuals give way to the

more popular process of compelling the nation
and the world to be good by statutory enactment.
He finds among Protestant ministers and their
leading laymen a new type of spiritual enthusiasm—though it is as old as Puritanism (older,
indeed) and seems new only because it has become as prevalent as an epidemic. He finds these
fervent followers of the new righteousness determined to mould all men in one pattern, and re-
solved, at any cost and with the expenditure of
any amount of force, to make it impossible for
other people to be sinners in their own way, while
blissfully unaware that bigotry, religious hatred
and pious cant may be worse sins than many of
the offenses already listed in the statute-books.

To return to the cause of my penitent confessions, take the present passion for social service.
Organized, as the welfare movement is, on a thoroughly professional and commercialized basis, it
has become one of the chief sins—and one of the
worst pests—in America to-day. No one could
possibly estimate the harm that has been done to
all movements for social betterment by the paid
uplifter. He is a general nuisance and many a good
cause has been ruined by his pernicious activity.
Nowhere has the evil of such commercialized service been more serious than in the churches. For
a time all of them were hypnotized into the en-
gagement of social-service "experts." These experts

were hired and fired. Most of them had to "make their own jobs" and in endeavoring to magnify their office they stuck busy fingers into other people's pies until the patience of the synods and conventions which engaged them was tried to the limit. Often they were parlor Socialists or doctrinaires who plunged their ecclesiastical organizations into unauthorized action in legislative halls and committed them to poorly digested programmes of social, economic and industrial reform. Ecclesiastical counsellors to State legislatures, amateur advisers in industrial relations and youthful critics of the present economic order were so numerous that one could not shake a stick at them collectively, much less hit them with it individually on the head. Among Protestant denominations of the more violent type paid secretaries and reform organizations became a menace as well as a nuisance. Good men have mourned over their activities and the people who are not naturally pious have been driven from indifference to bitter antagonism. They have engineered political blocs, forced through laws which only a small minority desired, held up legislation by demands for social and industrial reforms which could not be enforced. They have hung like hornets about the heads of legislators until the better type of politician has retired to private life and men of the baser sort have been pushed into the making of laws which they themselves do not obey and in whose real worth they have never had any faith.

The curse of commercialized service lies in the fact that most of us want to see necessary reforms enacted and necessary works of betterment performed; but paid experts who are obliged to magnify their office or lose it have defeated the very purpose of social service—first, by attempting so many things that nothing is done well and many things are attempted which ought not to be done at all; second, by increasing overhead expense through conventions, conferences, local and general offices and the multiplication of organization, until overlapping in work is the rule rather than the exception; and lastly, by making such exorbitant financial demands for all these things that the charitably disposed are giving up in despair.

We have come to a pass where it is almost impossible to get work done now unless some one is paid to do it. During the Great War there were so many paid workers doing every imaginable labor, from singing and dancing for the soldiers in camp to selling cigarettes and chocolate back of the front, that the tendency toward this commercializing of every social activity has been greatly strengthened. Thousands of earnest young women who did war work are now industriously engaged in discovering new openings for paid employment. Clergymen and laymen who were active or eloquent—for a price—are looking for secretarial positions with a worth-while salary attached. One cannot build a church or raise funds for charity without the aid of paid workers with standardized methods of enticing money from the purses of reluctant contributors, a large proportion of the money going into the pockets of the professional campaign directors. There are all sorts of organizations for civic betterment which furnish offices for paid executive secretaries, associations whose principal object is to offer advancement for professional city managers, additional social-service activities with paid workers treading on one another's toes.

II

The church has fallen victim to the vice of the age. We are standardizing religious education, standardizing parochial, synodical and diocesan organization, professionalizing parochial service and encouraging a numberless throng of would-be workers to learn the professional patter of the particular department in which they mean to offer their services—always at a price. In our way we are only a short distance behind the commercialized social-service workers who (for a salary) are busily engaged in proffering their panaceas for the remedy of social evils and hopefully advancing the approach of the social or industrial millennium.

Under the untiring prodding of the paid propagandist, church conventions have been made an occasion for the passage of resolutions advising everybody as to how everything should be done. The delegates were not chosen for any such exacting labors. They were chosen to see that the business of the church was done in a businesslike fashion—always a dull and drab and uninteresting task. When resolutions are passed about everything on earth, from child labor to the League of Nations, any one with half a brain knows that the men who pass the resolutions do not in any way represent their constituency as having been chosen for this particular educational and inspirational purpose. When Congress or State legislatures are flooded with appeals and resolutions from women's organizations, the members of these bodies—not being any bigger fools than most politicians— know that the resolutions were framed by a select little gathering of earnest and ignorant ladies of leisure, urged thereto by some paid enthusiast, and that the appeals and instructions represent a few more or less faithful attendants at club meetings and not the thousands of members for whom they claim to speak.

Because this is so, it is practically impossible to get serious attention for any serious proposal claiming popular support. Only when frightened legislators feel that a specially aggressive group holds the balance of power in a home district will they give heed to any plea—and the dictation to which they submit from these well-organized blocs results in the worst possible laws on the most impossible matters.

In my own church I have been entering my protests for several years. Alas! I have been abused. I can stand abuse; but what irks me is the fact that in spite of my usually fluent English, I have been grievously misunderstood. Of course the trouble with me is that in my pronouncements I have taken too much for granted in the way of intelligent interpretation. Like the good wife who said to her maid, "Mary, take the parrot away at once; Mr. Brown has lost his collar button," I did not feel it necessary to explain too minutely what was in my mind. It seemed best to leave something to the imagination. I now find that this was a mistake. Some people need to have everything elucidated amply and plainly in simple words of few syllables. They never can take anything for granted. They always want to be told in full detail what one means. It was right you should seek to dissemble your love; but why, they ask, why should you kick me down-stairs? I am now busy propelling some of the busybodies toward the door.

But let me explain. I am not seated in stolid contentment; like Gallio, caring for none of these things. I still care for them a lot. Only—I have come to the conclusion that "the trouble with the amateur carvers is that the gravy so seldom matches the wall-paper." Our social workers have been trying to cover too much territory and they have covered it with too many crude splashes.

As to my own grave disorder, let me confess, at the risk of unnecessary repetition, that the real trouble is that I am sick to death of circulars and appeals. I am not the only one who is complaining. Some one sent me the other day an eloquent outburst from another clergyman. He had discovered, like myself, that everybody who has a hobby, and is earnestly convinced that the adoption of his special nostrum would instantly usher in the millennium, at once feels moved to write either to the clergy or to the newspapers or to both. The message, of course, may occasionally be varied to suit the taste, and any given enthusiast may advocate any given nostrum, provided he or she observe two plain rules, viz.: first, not to advocate more than one nostrum at a time, since it is the special virtue of each to be an exclusive panacea; and, second, to make it quite clear that it is only the selfish indifference and inactivity of the clergy which is delaying the triumphant manifestation of the millennium.

Last week the ministerial mail-bag contained eight or ten such calls to service. If all had been heeded, no time would have been left in which to attend to any ordinary duties. It will not be necessary to enumerate these various calls—enough that they make one face the stubborn fact that one of the gravest perils that beset the clergy is the "restless scattering of our energies over an amazing multiplicity of interests; a scattering that leaves little margin of time for receptive and absorbing communion with God."

Worse than the plague of the mail-pouch is the curse of the early-morning telephone call. Even a saint of the placid type depicted in stained-glass windows would lose his temper if he lived in modern days, and during breakfast-time, or before, were called to the telephone morning after morning to take down fifty-word night letters. These urgent messages come from paid secretaries who are sending out a last appeal for aid in the Near East or a hurry call for an oriental hospital, or a request for the use of one's name on a petition to purify the movies, or an eleventh-hour summons to attend, and perchance address and pray for a conference of uplifters in a neighboring city. All of them good causes? Certainly. But why prejudice the cause by dragging its victim out of bed or away from the breakfast-table? Why not trust to the slower processes of the morning mail? Most men are not fit to live with until they have had a cup of strong coffee and a matutinal cigar. Then they are at peace with the world, fortified in spirit, kindly disposed toward all men. Then, if ever, they will meet with impaired power of resistance appeals to their purse, their patience or their piety. Even then, mails may annoy them, but they have not the same capacity to irritate as have the telephone and the telegraph message. Yet the expert secretary follows the methods of big business and telegraphs hither and yon at the expense of the office—and to the endangering of the souls of the impatient recipients of his messages.

Other secretaries specialize in besieging the minister with requests for the observance of new festivals in the Christian year. Mother's Day was the invention of a paid employee of the National Association of Florists, probably the same man who thought of the slogan, "Say it with flowers." Father and Son Week was probably a brilliant suggestion of the secretary of a clothiers' and haberdashers' club. Eat Oranges Week originated with an official of a California fruit-growers' association who earned a whole year's salary by thinking of this plan for increased consumption and remunerative production to meet the demand. Cleanup Week came from the Paint Manufacturers' publicity agent. Go to Church Sunday must have originated in the brain of a paid secretary of the committee in charge of the Back-sliders' Reunion.

There are also paid uplifters whose business it is to coax the clergy into every variety of preachment. A subject is easily at hand for every Sunday of the fifty-two on the calendar. He is asked to preach on purer plays, cleaner fiction, more innocuous movies. He may specialize as an oratorical advocate of the Red Cross or the Americanization Society. He may be a leader of the Boy Scouts, the Camp Fire Girls, the Knights of Sir Galahad, the Order of DeMolay, or the Sons and Daughters of I Will Arise. Sometimes he will believe in babies' welfare societies as the hope of America for the future; sometimes he may tend toward a firm faith in playgrounds for the numerous progeny of the foreign-born. By letter, telephone, telegraph or personal solicitation he will be urged to give inspirational addresses on the Y. M. C. A. swimming-pools, cafeterias for the Y. W., vacation camps, holiday houses, lessons in intensive dancing and a dozen other secular sacraments of modern Protestantism. All this, however, will be mild and inoffensive compared with the demands made upon him to give undivided allegiance to the varied programme of social reform, with conferences to be held, petitions to be circulated, public officials to be bedeviled and congregations urged to supply funds to carry on the ambitious projects.

III

Now, the ordinary minister, we have been told, makes up for not being very wise by being really quite exceptionally well-meaning. Like the peasant in Æsop's fable, he is very desirous of pleasing every one. Hence he neglects his proper work— and no one will convince me that he hasn't a work properly his—becomes a smatterer in political economy and sociology, preaches earnestly (and inaccurately) about many isms, and positively exudes the spirit of the uplift. Unfortunately it takes a long time to become an expert, and the life of any particular ism is usually short. Hence by the time the minister has neglected his flock long enough to speak with authority on any one thing, should that time ever arrive, he finds that something else has taken its place.

The average American clergyman is really not a hypocrite. He is an earnest soul seeking to do good, often not having a very clear idea as to how he may do the good he seeks to do, apt to excuse his failure on the ground that his ecclesiastical superiors lack in leadership, anxious therefore to have a paid expert tell him how and where he may become active in uplifting his fellow men, and in the pathetic ignorance of his heart following every new fad in the fond expectation of satisfying his soul's desire. Do not be too hard on

him. He means well. He is really deserving of
more credit than the cynic who smiles at his halting efforts.

But—he is tiresome, excessively so. Perhaps I
would best say that I am quite aware that all of
us—we of the clergy—are apt to be tiresome in
our moral enthusiasms. I wish we could retain our
enthusiasm while at the same time ceasing to be
fanatical. If the paid uplifters would let us alone,
I am sure we would soon become pleasant people
to live with. Indeed, I flatter myself that some
may be such, even as things are.

In the meanwhile, it is our misfortune that our
very moral enthusiasms make us an easy prey for
the professional propagandists. That is why we get
so excited over the industrial democracy that we
are on the point of dividing our incomes—which
are not large enough to be heavily taxed—among
the proletariat, only to discover (alas! too late)
that we have spent our little all on postage-stamps
and stationery carrying on a correspondence in
response to the cyclone of circulars that sweeps
upon us like the western gales of incoming March.
That is why we are engaged in the task of outlaw-
ing war. We are the victims of paid pacifists who
induce us to preach disarmament in season and
out and demand the abolition of armies and navies
at once, instead of trying out the experiment on
a small scale and beginning by discharging the

local police force and throwing away the key to the front door. We all hate war—who does not, save a few benighted followers of an insane Polish philosopher? But the secretary of some peace society has induced us to inscribe our names to a resolution that the only way to avoid war is by action analogous to that of tying our hands and letting a bad man hit our children.

But I have drifted far afield, skipping from cause to cause as inconsequently as the uplifters themselves. Natural indignation has led me to visualize the whole welfare movement in its various ramifications. What I originally set out to do was to enter a protest against the prevalent tendency to resolve religion into nothing other than terms of social activity and trust to successive schemes of legislation for the reformation of society and the salvation of the human race. One need but read the history of legislation for the past two decades, in all its paternalistic progress, to discover how one programme after another has been enacted into law; how each has fallen short of its promised perfections; how the eager experts have promptly organized new movements, bound to bring a little closer the dawn of the new day; how each in turn has failed to produce the anticipated results; how the multiplicity of laws has led to contempt for law, and how deep-rooted is the idea that all this is the real province of religion and support of it the real duty of all who profess and call themselves Christians.

So the churches go gaily on toward the millennium and the propagandists daily show them new tasks to accomplish preparatory to its coming. Sometimes, here and there, an earnest worker becomes weary, but there is always near at hand a paid secretary to prod him to his feet again. Meanwhile, on with the dance—and damned be he who first cries, "Hold! Enough!" Let us do the welfare fox-trot till we lose our breath or bust. When a leisure hour comes I am thinking of writing a paper about it for one of the clerical brotherhoods. It will be entitled "The Present Decay in Religion; or, the Activity of the Clergy in Every Good Work." There may be a second paper (if I escape alive after the first one) on "Spasmodic Preachments and their Relation to Religious Hysteria."

What gives some of us anxiety is that the work of social reform has been gaily taken up by faddists who make it such a joke and themselves such a public pest that almost every good cause is handicapped and serious people cannot get a hearing. As I have already intimated, there is hardly a public man of any position who does not discount every appeal made on behalf of better social legislation by attributing the demand to the sentimental fancy of the reformer and seeing in it no real expression of public opinion. For the matter of that, is there actually any force of public opinion behind many of the proposed reforms? Such a public sentiment can be aroused; it has been aroused. But it will never be aroused by men and women who follow a will-o'-the-wisp of reform, led by a starry-eyed secretary who is well paid for his activities. And it will not be exerted continuously and effectively under the leadership of those whose one idea seems to be that you can legislate people into paradise and that a law once on the statute-books becomes *ipso facto* a self-operating piece of reform machinery.

Particularly, and by way of emphatic repetition, in social work, as in politics, we need to concentrate. There is such a babel of sound now from the advocates of reform—women in particular—that most people depart before they find out what it is all about, like the Oriental visitor who attended a concert and (under the mistaken impression that the music was over) left before it began, only to discover afterward that he had heard the orchestra tuning up. And the pace has been so fast, the race so furious. It looks sometimes as if we had not stayed long enough in our hurried welfare journey; we have not remained at any one station long enough to hear the echoes of the whistle of the departing train on which we came.

Meanwhile, there are thousands of honest-hearted clergy who are not hopelessly inefficient. Thousands of us, at any rate, believe that we have escaped the vulgarity and blatancy of the many Main Streets of America. We know that religious impressions must find active expression in service and in a stumbling fashion we are trying to show others how and where their religious activities may be directed. The excessively energetic paid helpers who are so eager to help us bore us to tears because they really obstruct our efforts.

Meanwhile, also, it is my honest conviction that the clergyman has a work peculiarly his own, and that if this work is not done all the work of other men will be in vain. Every social reformer must feel that his work is hindered by the faults of individuals. Every student of economics knows that his problems are partly moral. Every political reformer recognizes that the first need of a nation is good men; really good men—men of honest purpose—not men who can talk so eloquently about goodness that as they soar into the blue empyrean the stars reverberate with their oratory.

IV

The only solution that has thus far suggested itself to my conscience, when the field-secretaries have given me time to think, is to let somebody else do something.

That does not mean that I am going to preach to others and call them to labor while I am idle and indifferent. Every layman should be interested and active in good works, but we do not expect him entirely to neglect his business or professional affairs in order to show his social zeal. Why can't the minister follow the same plan?

Then, second, as I do not expect to do everything myself, so I shall not expect other people to do more than myself. And therefore I shall not look for the accomplishment of the whole social programme all at once. I am going to reason with my friends and try to induce them to discharge a few paid workers and restrain their own zeal. I am going to urge them to alight at one station and stay there awhile. Some of them don't know where they are going—they only know they are on their way. Others are so torn between conflicting welfare movements that they are like the east-bound traveller on the New York Central who walked in his sleep just before the train pulled into Albany and awoke only to find himself on the way to Boston while his clothes were headed for New York. I am going to urge my zealous friends to go somewhere and stay put, though I have very little expectation that they will accept my advice.

Finally, even at the risk of making myself somewhat of a bore in doing it, I mean to keep on insisting that religion is something finer and more

attractive than the blatant and vulgar substitute
for it which obsesses America at the present time.
I am not naturally critical or pessimistic; my
friends say that I am occasionally cheery and
sweet-tempered. But the best of dispositions will
soon be ruined if one discovers that, just because
one is a clergyman, the man in the street classes
one with the religionists of American Protestantism. I worship a different God from theirs, I am
sure. If religion meant the abominable thing it
must mean to irritated victims and observers of
this crude American caricature of it, I would have
nothing to do with it myself, nor would I blame
others if they denounced it with contempt. I am
driven to desperation at the thought that (because
I wear a clerical collar) the uplifters are making
a laughing-stock of me as well as of themselves.

Therefore I shall keep on teaching what I believe to be real religion. Though its quiet voice
may not be heard now, as the trumpets blare insistently for more constitutional amendments,
more statutory enactment; and more welfare
movements, I still believe that it has attractive
power and that the day may not be far distant
when men will once more recognize its modest
charm. A few hundred kindly, courteous, quiet,
well-disposed churchmen in a community—all of
them minding their own business and modestly
and unobtrusively worshipping and serving God

in their own way; not obnoxiously insistent that everybody shall serve and worship God in exactly the same way; in particular, not impertinently inquisitive as to the faults and failings of others, nor overzealous to bring them to repentance, and a better life—a few hundred decent, old-fashioned Christians of this type will do more for the good of their fellow men than all the leaders of all the Hi Ys in all this glorious land of the (alleged) free and home of the brave.

THE CHURCH AND THE LAW:
A PROTEST

THE CHURCH AND THE LAW:
A PROTEST

I

A WELL-KNOWN Washington newspaper correspondent recently addressed a remonstrance to the ministers of America. He urged them to stay at home themselves, and to keep at home all clerical lobbyists, professional uplifters, and ministerial engineers of "politico-moral blocs." He added that, in his opinion, the clergy in general, and especially the ministers of Protestant churches and their constituency, were making themselves a general nuisance and bringing religion into contempt by organizing themselves into a Society for Petitioning Congress. "The prestige of organized Christianity as a persuasive force," he declared, "has through such activity received a blow from which it will not soon recover."

This protest, somewhat humorous and exaggerated, is symptomatic of a return to sanity and sense which may be observed among intelligent Christians, even though the Anti-Saloon League, the Christian pacifists, the social reformers and the ladies of leisure who function through women's clubs and church societies still besiege the legislative halls of the state and the nation with repeated appeals and pronunciamentos.

It may be worth while, therefore, to ask just what the duty of the Christian church really is, in questions of social reform. Recent discussions of the vexed prohibition question—in particular, certain differences of opinion in connection with the survey made by the Federal Council of the Churches of Christ in America, and other surveys by the Moderation League—show the need of such clear thinking as to the true function of the church in advancing human welfare. There are hopeful signs that many enthusiastic supporters of recent legislation are beginning to cherish healthy doubts as to the wisdom of changing the church's charter and making it, to repeat a phrase, a moral policeman instead of a moral teacher. The failure of prohibition in many sections of the country is at least halting the moral reformers of America in the agitation of further efforts through statutory enactment to impose their own standards upon all men and invoke the aid of the civil authority in support of their own ethical code. An increasing number of people have begun to see that moral reform, if it is to be permanent and effective, must come from within; it cannot be imposed from without.

Let it be said, at once, that those who believe the churches should not go into politics are not

necessarily intransigent upholders of an individualistic gospel. Of course, the church must concern itself not only with the salvation of individuals, but with all conditions that surround and
affect individuals. If its voice is silent about matters of public welfare here and now, it will not be
listened to in proclaiming a gospel of future good
—the peace and joy of a world to come. It is true,
without question, that mere philanthropic effort,
without the inspiration, motive force, and sus-
taining power of a deep religious faith, will not
meet the needs of human life. While the church's
message, therefore, must always be an evangelical
message, the church must also be the conscience
of the community. Its mission is not solely to proclaim a gospel of pardon and peace and to be the
administrant of sacraments of grace. It has social
obligations and a prophetic mission for its own
time. "Preaching the old gospel" must mean presenting the old truth in a new setting, the old
message of the kingdom for the new age, the vital
teaching of the Master vitally applied to present
problems. The supreme need of the age is for men
who have the wisdom, the courage, and the conscience to guide the Christian forces of the country in making thorough application of the principles of the Gospel to the conditions of every-day
life and the needs of our modern social and industrial system. Back of every economic and indus-

trial question there lies usually a moral principle.
The church is the guardian of morals. Surely,
therefore, it is incumbent upon the church's members to concern themselves about the solution of
public questions. Only so can the Christian fulfil
more completely the obligation of the second great
Gospel commandment, to love our neighbor as
ourselves. Only so will he show—not that he is his
brother's keeper, but that he is something better,
his brother's brother.

It is the glory of our day that this obligation
for the proclamation of corporate righteousness
and public morality, as well as the call to private
and individual consecration, has been accepted
whole-heartedly. We see clearly the need of a
church with a living message for the present day.
Men will never again be interested in a religion
which is tremendously exercised over small things
and passive about the needs of humanity. We have
moved far and fast since the day when it could be
said that, for the most part, church-members were
holding themselves aloof from the things which
vitally move men; offering religion labelled and
bottled, prescribed for old people, invalids, and
children. The men of to-day may not be able to
express themselves very clearly, but they have an
instinctive feeling that the church's voice should
be heard as a directive influence in public matters.
They want the church to do more than generalize

in morals; they want it in some way to be specific, as were the prophets of old.

Feeling all this, many men both inside the church and without, whose consciences have been quickened to the need of a social gospel, are impatient for the church to speak emphatically on the problems to which they are giving their best thought and prayer. Are they deeply moved by problems of injustice—they want the church to stand out boldly in support of their economic remedy. Are they concerned with the social sin—they want the church to get behind their particular legislative enactments. Are they trying to crush the liquor power—they demand that the corporate influence of the church shall be used in favor of the particular solution of the evil which they propose. They are impatient to have all these things made a part of the church's "articles of religion."

All my own natural sympathies are with them. I dislike to seem too unsympathetic, much less to throw a wet blanket over their projects, or in any way to chill their enthusiasm. We most of us feel that the church must do something for the great purposes they have in view. That, of course, is undeniable. Therefore the question is not, shall we do anything? not, shall the church do anything? But—what shall it do, and how shall it do it? We must be careful lest we deny the social enthusiast our support. We must be careful, on the other hand, of a too hasty acceptance of all that he asks the church to do in the way of support.

II

What is the Gospel reply to this impatient call to the church to do something? Surely no one ever had a keener sympathy for social needs than the Lord Jesus Christ himself. No one ever showed greater fearlessness in the presence of long-intrenched wrong-doing in matters social and political. He cleansed the temple of the petty grafters who had, for their own profit, rented out the sacred enclosure—and he paid the penalty with his life. He rebuked the social injustice of the Pharisees who devoured widows' houses—and their enmity was the first step that led to the final penalty. He made his home with the poor. He knew their problems and felt their pains and anxieties. He came from Galilee—and Galilee was the home of radicals. He was the friend of publicans and sinners, and he knew all the ugly story of the social evil. His Gospel was the Gospel of the Kingdom, of a perfect reign of righteousness on the earth, of a complete acceptance everywhere of social responsibility and social obligation. He surely was alive to social needs.

And yet, instead of legislating on them, he

showed a singular reticence against that very course. He was not, in the strict sense of the word, a social reformer. Instead of urging legislation or preaching social revolution, he contented himself with arousing a new conscience that would itself gradually solve the problems. Indeed, the strength and power of his work lay in this very fact, that he declined to advocate specific reforms. He did something better: he set forth large principles which made reform inevitable. It is a distinction, perhaps, which is difficult to make clear in connection with the church's duty to-day; yet it is a real distinction.

No man of this generation has been more keen for organized Christianity to support a social gospel and proclaim a public morality than the late Bishop Williams, of Michigan. He was courageous to the last degree in his own utterances. Yet once when he was speaking in Ford Hall, and an enthusiastic radical in the audience demanded that his church should "get behind the Socialist programme," he very rightly replied that it was not the business of the church to advocate any political or economic measure. If it would fulfil its mission it must be the home of men of many minds. The church must be at least as comprehensive as Ford Hall, he said, where there were gathered together in a forum men of widely differing views, presumably all interested in making better conditions in society, industry, and politics. The church's business is to inspire men with such a common motive, to create in them the spirit of brotherhood and service. Though men will always differ as to methods, if enough men get the right spirit almost any method will work.

I do not know of any illustration that will bring out more clearly what I mean than one from the life of Henry George. When he was conducting his campaign for the mayoralty in New York, he was introduced at a labor-union meeting in Cooper Institute as "The friend of the workingman." Stepping to the front of the stage, he began: "That word of introduction misrepresents me; I am not the friend of the workingman." There was a hush of astonishment before he added: "I am not the friend of the capitalist. I am for men, simply men as men, regardless of accidental distinction of race, creed, color, class, or employment." In other words, Mr. George was recognized as the champion of the poor; he felt that his economic programme would solve the problem of poverty; yet he wished to avoid any entanglements which would make him merely a class representative.

Hysterical appeals are often heard now, summoning the church to do just what Mr. George refused to do. To accept the challenge and unqualifiedly to obey the summons would range the church on the side of class antagonism and class hatred.

III

So it is with numerous other platforms and programmes the church is asked to support. Organized Christianity would lose its real place of power if it accepted the challenge. No, the paramount social duty of the church is not the planning and engineering of economic schemes, not the formulating of programmes; but the enlargement of sympathy and the realization of fellowship among men; the kindling of brotherly confidence and understanding, and the spreading of it as by contagion. The real business of the church is to make men's hearts right, and then trust their enlightened consciences somehow to solve their civic duty. In other words, the church cannot (in its corporate capacity) pass upon many such problems, because when it comes to programmes and parties, when we deal with economic, industrial, and educational systems, even when we frame health regulations and liquor laws, good Christians have a perfect right to disagree as to details.

Let me re-emphasize what I have said before. I may believe in prohibition; you may be conscientiously opposed to it, or doubtful of its ex-

pediency. I may be a single-taxer, you a socialist.
You and I may believe that government owner-
ship of public utilities or general necessities of
life is the only remedy for certain forms of op-
pression; another man may wholly disagree with
us. The church may, through social-service commissions or expert moral surveys, investigate all
these questions, try to give us information, seek
to keep us alive to their importance, help to form
our opinion, inspire us to work. If we disapprove,
we may turn out our experts or commissions and
get others. But we cannot turn out the church!
And the church oughtn't to turn us out! And,
therefore, so long as we may conscientiously differ,
the church has no right to pledge any of us by
legislation or resolution. It must be at least as
comprehensive as Ford Hall.

These are principles which would have saved
us many a sorrow had they been remembered
in the days when we were launched on our prohibition crusade. Of course, the provocation to abol-
ish the saloon was great. Brewers and distillers
have only themselves to blame for the destruction
of their industry. The saloon, allied as it was with
politics and vice, cried to high heaven for reform,
and the financial interests behind it only flouted
the public demand for such reform and regulation. For the most part, Christian people saw the
real work of the church. Patient teaching was

gradually changing the morals of the nation in the matter of excessive drinking. I well remember the day when every buyer who came to the city was provided with all he wished to drink, and then taken "down the line," if he so desired. All that changed. Drunkenness was no longer a good joke; it was disgusting and revolting. Not only was it not a good joke; it was not good business. Almost every travelling man knew that he could not succeed unless he kept sober and lived straight.

Then, out of the pernicious political corruption of the blinded liquor interests, arose the activity of the Anti-Saloon League, and churches became party organizations, led by skilled ecclesiastical politicians, and condoning practices quite as objectionable as any indulged in by politicians of the common or garden variety.

The result was the Eighteenth Amendment— welcomed in some sections of the country, received in astonishment in others, foisted upon not a few States, and even where favorable sentiment was strongest, accepted because it was supposed to be the only possible method of curbing the power of the saloon. It is needless to argue about its good results or its bad effects. Much may be said on both sides. Much that has been said is the voice of partisan opinion. The one point I would make is this: that the whole subject should be reconsidered in the light of experience and in con-

scientious desire to decide charitably without bigotry or bias.

IV

Because the problem we wish to solve is a problem of civil authority, good Christians may hold
widely differing views as to the wisdom of recent
legislation—and be good Christians still. Let me
classify some who are sincere, conscientious, consecrated Christians, though others would rule them
out.

First, there are those who believe that the State
has no right to interfere with their personal pref-
erence in the matter of alcoholic drink, because
Jesus Christ did not declare the use of such bever-
age a sin—on the contrary, actually used fermented wine in the institution of the Holy Communion. Few would go so far, but (though I
hardly care myself to fight for the right to take a
drink!) there are actually some who feel so
strongly that the Volstead Act is a lie and a tyran-
nical piece of legislation that they justify dis-
obedience of it. Some there are who honestly believe this legislation unchristian in spirit—an ex-
hibition of modern Manichæan thought which
finds evil in material things rather than in the
heart of man. Shall we banish all such from the
Christian fellowship, or make their stay so uncomfortable that they feel obliged to depart of
their own accord? Dare we do this if they sin-

cerely believe that their position is loyal to their
Lord's teaching?

Second, there are those who feel that even if
the government (by way of health regulation)
may interfere with personal liberty to the extreme
of absolute prohibition, it is a fatal mistake to
impose such a law on the whole nation, because
the will of one section attempts in this way to
dictate to another part of the country a rule which
by no possibility or probability can be enforced.
Certainly, such an opinion as to a question of
legislative wisdom ought not to be made the butt
of bigoted vituperation.

Third, there are those who feel that extreme
legislation is to be deplored because, in spite of
the good the law has accomplished, it has made
drinking conditions worse than before, even if
limiting the number of drinkers, has increased
the use of strong distilled liquors (often dangerous and poisonous) especially among the young,
has contributed to the increase of lawlessness, is
class legislation favoring the rural parts as against
the industrial classes, and has enormously fostered official corruption. Some who are of this
opinion are convinced total abstainers themselves,
certainly are now strict observers of the law. Shall
they be denounced as immoral "wets" for whom
there is no place in the society of faithful church
members?

Fourth, there are those who feel that the whole

method of reform by statutory enactment is
wrong, and that continued talk about enforcement
is idle, because no one would dare demand the
enormous appropriations and the huge army of
enforcement officers necessary to compel obedience in some parts of the country, or engage to
keep the army (or navy) of enforcement reasonably uncorrupt, even if there were money avail-
able for their employment. Such considerations
lead them to feel that laws of this particular kind
are always doubtful means of moral improvement.
Laws cannot be enforced save as they express rea-
soned public opinion. If public opinion is strong
enough, it can mould men's habits without laws
as well as with them; if there is not a strong
enough public sentiment, habits cannot be regulated, however many laws the statute-books may
contain. This argument may sound absurd to intense moral-uplifters, but who shall say that those
who use it are not conscientious, even though mis-
guided? Wherein can their error be made a reason
for their excommunication, or for driving them
into self-excommunication?

V

Thus we come to the original contention, that
the supreme sin of modern Phariseeism is the sin
of dependence upon the civil arm for the regula-

tion of morals. The Pharisees were the good people of their day—only they were so sure of their goodness, and so convinced of the worth of their regulatory system, that they enforced it on others, and in doing so became hardened in self-righteousness. Jesus Christ's teaching came as fresh and vital truth to men who were lost in the maze of such religious machinery.

The church must go back to the method of its Lord—reform and renew men by the winsomeness and attractiveness of his teaching, instead of compelling them to behave by reliance on the civil arm. Some things we have been doing which we never should have attempted, and because we have tried them we are losing our moral influence. Men sneer at our amateur efforts, and laugh at our hysterical parsons, or become annoyed or even angry at our theoretical pronouncements and leave us alone.

The prohibition question has aroused so generally a bitterness of controversy that it is difficult to make men see, in connection with the subject, the soundness of this view of the function of Christian citizenship. One or two other examples, briefly glanced at, may make the thought clear.

I know of many a modest American who would rejoice to see an army of churchmen march upon the national capital and declare in no uncertain language that war is unchristian. Yet most of us would object to their framing that indisputable statement into a law of extreme pacifism. We know, in our hearts, that war will cease only when the spirit of Christ has more really dominated nations as well as individuals, so that national rivalries and misunderstandings shall give place to mutual good-will. Meanwhile we are not prepared to cancel appropriations for the army and navy, any more than we would favor the effort to check the crime wave by discharging the local police force.

Practically, all of us want America to do all that is possible to serve the world; in the days after Versailles surely we all wanted to do our best for a distracted world. But there were some millions of Americans, the majority of them Christians, who resented a particular method of service to humanity, and with glad acclaim voted for the party which opposed our entering the League of Nations. I had difficulty in expressing my convictions as to their mental processes or their political bigotries in truly pious phrases; but I never thought of indignant denunciation such as would practically read them out of the church.

I myself would like to see a clear enunciation of the fact that any industrial autocracy violates the spirit of Christian brotherhood, but I am quite sure that I do not want any clergyman to tell me just exactly what laws he thinks will solve the

complicated economic and industrial problems of
the day. When I hear some earnest and enthusiastic clergymen preaching, and listen to their pronouncements on capital and labor, I wonder that
employers use as mild language as that in which
they usually do express their conviction that the
minister may be a devout pastor but when he de-
parts from the sphere of pastoral service may show
himself also as a consummate ass.

All of which shows that most of us, unless the
question be one where our own prejudices make
us cocksure, do feel that there is a clear distinction between moral teaching and the particular
political, social, industrial, economic, or legislative method by which the moral teaching may be
applied to particular problems of our complex
modern life. The churches of late have failed to
make this distinction, to the hurt of their real influence. They must be called back to their real
duty—which is the supplying of the spiritual
dynamic that shall make men strong enough and
brave enough to follow the path of truth and
right, no matter where it may lead or what it may
cost, to think unselfishly and labor courageously
amid all the problems of citizenship, so that they
may be solved in accordance with Christian principles and in the spirit of Christ himself. One
thing, and one thing only, and one thing always,
the church ought to do, and I make this protest

to call it back to that task. It is this: To induce us all to think of our citizenship, to make us all deeply prayerful in facing its duties and responsibilities, to make us profoundly conscientious in the exercise of its privileges, to give us all a right motive, to fill us with determination not to shirk our obligations, to charge us with spiritual energy to labor unceasingly not for our individual salvation only, but for our country's welfare and our neighbor's good.

Above all else, the clear call comes to American Protestants of to-day to exercise their Christian citizenship in a spirit of gracious liberality and sympathetic understanding of those who cannot see with them, eye to eye. I may not read aright the thoughts of those who are outside the Christian fold, but my impression is that they are becoming hardened in an opposition to organized Christianity by the feeling that it does not really represent the spirit of the Master. They were once outside because they were doubtful or questioning. They are now determined to stay outside because they find the methods of Protestant Christianity distasteful and repellent.

THE CHURCH'S LOSS OF PRESTIGE

THE CHURCH'S LOSS OF PRESTIGE

I

THERE are times when one is a little ashamed to be known as a clergyman. I like to take off my clerical collar and travel in mufti, sitting in the smoking compartment and taking part in the spontaneous conversation of a group of men who do not feel that they are under restraint because of the censorious and accusatory presence of a parson.

Of course I am not really ashamed of the ministry; I rejoice in it and cannot imagine myself content with any other profession. What shames me is the thought that my companions have a conception of the ministry which, if they but knew it, is actually as absurd and abhorrent to me as it is to them. They do not discriminate. I know how they are classifying me, and the knowledge is far from pleasant. I am not ashamed of the ministry itself; I am ashamed to be identified with that which the other men in the smoking compartment conceive it to be. In the back of their heads is the conviction that most ministers are engaged in snooping into other people's business, regulating other people's morals, and endeavoring

71

to standardize other people's brains. They regard all ministers alike as professional members of the Society of Moral Uplifters. They conceive of the ministerial life as narrow, if not bigoted, as joyless and severe, censorious, rigid, inflexible in its prejudices, ignorant in its criticisms, ungenerous in its judgments, petty in its aims.

The average business man knows of an occasional member of the ministerial profession whom he acclaims as different: a "good mixer," a "go-getter," a "he-man," the friend of Rotarians and Kiwanians. One wonders whether down in the bottom of his heart he really does respect this other type of parson whom he so exuberantly praises. At any rate, there are lots of other people who do not like him. Perhaps the modern Babbitt of the pulpit repels more men than his supposedly gloomy brother. Israel, we are told, lost its place and power as a nation because it forsook God and rejected His revelation; but the Jewish hierarchy at its worst never fell so low as have some of the up-and-coming preachers of America. Read the advertised subjects of the Sunday sermons in many Protestant churches, or the announcements on the bulletin-boards, read the ecclesiastical electric-light signs on not a few church buildings that have begun a mild rivalry of the Great White Way, and then remember that even in the days of Annas and Caiphas there were no billboards in Jerusalem announcing a "Grand Sacrifice in the Temple," with prize-fed bulls and goats and lambs, expert priests to slaughter them, Herod's String Band advertised to assist, or trumpeters from Pilate's Bodyguard, all heralded in the flaring invitation: "Come to the Temple. Come to the Sacrifice. Hear the Augmented Choir of Levites. Come and Worship the Lord God Almighty."

The 100-per-cent American may not mind it, though actually I suspect that he has occasional glimpses into his own mental processes sufficiently illuminating to suggest that he may have less admiration than we suppose for his ministerial imitator. Even if he does not object to the publicity stunts of the modern minister, there are many others (and these the very people most worth bringing into the service of religion) who do mind. Nor is that all. These latter object to many other things. They object to the professionally managed evangelistic and financial campaigns of the churches; their sense of religious values is offended at the excessive emphasis on all highly organized plans for money raising, even though it be for such altruistic objects as missionary funds; they are irritated at the professional patter of the field secretaries who manage the canvass; their reverence revolts at "selling religion" or (even worse) "selling Jesus Christ"; they do not want to think of God as a Magnified Rotarian, nor are they ever likely to be enamoured of a religion that has lost all sense of mystery, has no feeling of awe, is never hushed into solemn silence, substitutes for devotion a breezy familiarity with God and holy things, and goes about the business of salvation with an effrontery which is really indicative of spiritual poverty and an utter lack of appreciation of what St. Paul called "the mystery of godliness."

Although the worst of the "go-getters" are now leaving Christian pulpits for secretarial positions, the church suffers none the less. They are busily engaged in torch-bearing in many directions. Some of them are agents of reform organizations; some are encamped in State capitals or at Washington; some content themselves with peripatetic engagements at women's clubs and business men's organizations; some are downing demons of drink and lust and indecency or inveighing against the manners and morals of youth—and in consequence are much more in evidence than their brethren who continue in a more localized service.

I was saying something like this to a group of sympathetic listeners the other day, when two of them, both college graduates, broke forth simultaneously upon me with their own objections. One of them was still agitated over Dayton and evolution—which led me to believe that he had not been indulging in much laborious intellectual effort during his first year out of college, else he would have known the general attitude of the clergy. The other was an older man, engaged since graduation in social and educational work. Both despised the men of the ministry because to the irritation of the first critic, they were (to quote) "hopelessly behind the age," "ignorant of the science they attack," and "uninterested or unintelligent as to modern problems, social, industrial, educational," according to the other; men who condemn books they have never read, criticise theories they have never examined, excoriate evils of which they have had no practical knowledge, or indulge in "commonplace pronouncements" and "platitudinous praise of outworn beliefs." Here I held up my hands and humbly apologized for havmg opened the subject with any feeble protests of my own.

All of which, however, explains the feeling that occasionally moves me to travel incognito and conceal my ministerial occupation. For, honestly, I do not believe I am any of the things which this varied group abhor and with which I naturally dislike to be too closely identified. And I am equally sure that there is a saving remnant among the clergy who, just as certainly as myself, are caricatured by any such descriptions.

II

Of course it is absurd to be sensitive about it. It would be just as sensible to conceal the fact of one's Christian belief because others have failed to understand what Christianity is. For unquestionably they do fail to understand. I have talked with students in the enlightened precincts of Princeton and Yale who seem to think that acceptance of a creed gives precisely the same importance to the fact of the Resurrection as to certain theories about it—indeed, sometimes it appears that they regard the fact of the Resurrection and the recorded estimate of the cubic displacement of Noah's Ark as equally vital credal requirements in the ministry. There comes to my mind the remark of a presumably intelligent young student at Cornell whose thorough study of Christian truth had led him to reject it because, as he triumphantly declared, it was impossible that Joshua could have caused the sun to stand still. He listened in open-mouthed amazement when I told him that the statement was a quotation from a book of poetry and that poets had never yet been able to describe events in the humdrum language of every-day life. I have met other youthful members of the *intelligentsia* who still think that Christianity is invalidated by the story

of Jonah's somewhat cramped living quarters, unaware that there are parables in the Old Testament as well as in the Gospels.

One would hardly believe that it could be possible in these days to find intelligent people hark-
ing back to Biblical difficulties which agitated
men in the age of Ingersoll; nor is it easy to believe that the church-school teaching, which at
least a few of these young people must have received, could leave them so hopelessly ignorant
and out of date. Perhaps they were "stringing"
the parson. Yet so uninformed is the average man
as to the real content of the Christian faith, that
he is astonished to be told that we also are
"anxious not to be obscurantists, but to live in
the light of modern knowledge," and that we are
trying to disentangle religion from antiquated
ideas. Most of us place our whole emphasis on the
fact of Christ's own life and teaching. The core of
Christianity is its belief that "the heart of God
is as the heart of Jesus." We find in the life of
Christ strength to hold fast our faith in God in
spite of the cruelties of this machinelike world of
ours, with all its seeming blind fatality. The critic
does not know that some of us who have studied
modern science and psychology feel that the universe is not a "closed mechanism." We have what
George Tyrrell called "faith in long trousers" and
have long since ceased to be contented with mere

"faith in knickerbockers." We are trying to show the beauty of the gospel story of the Christ who brought God to men in the glory of a new discovery. A college pastor recently told me that any knowledge of the facts of Christianity was so rare among students that the supreme literary need in his work was a simple life of Christ, written in vivid form, that could be read in an hour.

Nor does the average man understand the essential spiritual qualities of Christian living. Doctor Maude Royden wrote recently of a conversation with a distinguished theologian to whom she exclaimed impulsively, "I hate religious people," to which he replied, "Shake hands! So do I." Then she explained with illuminating clearness that she does not actually dislike really religious people, but that Christian graces must be founded on every-day virtues, and were built on the basis of these natural virtues by Jesus Christ. What repels the modern world is the fact that so many Christians supposed to be living the life of grace do not first practise the every-day virtues of ordinarily decent people. The attractiveness of Christ's life and teaching arises out of the fact that he assumes the presence of these natural virtues before attempting to inculcate the higher ideals of holiness and devotion. "Christ had strength of character, courage of mind and body, great physical courage as well as great moral courage. In Him

every Christian grace was founded upon the rock
of honor and loyalty, courage and justice, a pierc-
ing vision, a great strength." Many people who
criticise the Christian religion have never taken
the pains to find out what it really is.

If the facts of Christianity are so little known,
and the teaching of Christianity so little understood, that is no excuse for the Christian to conceal his own faith; it is a challenge to him to explain it, much more is it a challenge to try to live
it, and by the attractiveness of his own life commend it to others.

Likewise, if the ministry is so often caricatured
by those who have had unpleasant experiences of
ministerial vices, is not that a challenge to fly
one's own colors? Why not try to show that
"there are others"? Indeed, why expect that all
who profess and call themselves Christians are
sure to be beautiful examples of the faith they
are supposed to have accepted? If Christianity
is so often misunderstood, even by those who profess it, why expect that its ministers may not
sometimes be blind leaders of the blind? If I am
occasionally ashamed to be classed with some
of the amazingly vulgar or amazingly ignorant
preachers of the day, have I not often been a bit
anxious lest I should be classed with some Americans? After a time, we all come to our senses and
realize how unjust is the ready condemnation of

a nation because of the unlovely characteristics of some of our compatriots. We groan or chuckle over American-drawn portraits of our Babbitts and are condescendingly superior in our judgments of the Main Streets of America, and then we remember that there are many fine characters living quietly and modestly in American homes not unlike those of Gopher Prairie, and many generous public-spirited men rendering community service with unselfish and even self-sacrificing devotion among the membership of the much despised luncheon clubs of America—men who are doing their level best, even though they wear name plates on their coat lapels, men who hate hypocrisy as heartily as the smart writers who criticise them, who may occasionally look silly in their clumsy efforts to satisfy their longings for comradeship and good-fellowship, and yet are no more absurd in their antics than their cynical critics; men who really believe in the worth of commonplace things, who are democratic at heart, free from affectation and snobbery, and honestly anxious to give everybody a fair chance and a square deal. Away, then, with the hyper-critics! Why should we judge American business men by the occasional crudities of an Exchange Club orator or a guest of the Lions? And why judge the ministry by flowers of *Americana* plucked in obscure pastures? Some of the clerical gentlemen

are rather poor specimens, but not many of them
are as bad as some of them occasionally are.

III

Nevertheless, it cannot seriously be disputed
that the ministry has fallen into public disregard
and that the churches have decidedly lost prestige.
Why?

Here in America for many reasons. Sect rivalry
has given us numerous weak little congregations
with a poorly equipped ministry. The possibility
of effective service in these organizations is so
small that the finest type of men are not often
enough attracted to the clerical office and when
they do come even the best of them sometimes
grow discouraged and disheartened. This means
an almost inevitable loss of ideals—the minister
slips back intellectually, spiritually, even morally.
Only the strongest can stand firm against the
general down-grade tendency.

Sect rivalry, moreover, emphasizes certain doctrines and practices which were never essentials
of the faith, and ministers spend their time incul-
cating teachings, upholding standards of social
conduct, or defending ecclesiastical judgments
which should have been abandoned long ago. The
multitude of rival sects makes for a narrow de-

nominationalism, in some places bigoted in the extreme.

Elsewhere, in the revulsion against the crudities and eccentricities of denominational teaching, there has developed a false liberality which has emasculated Christianity. In the days of the Roman Empire, Chesterton reminds us, the world nearly died of broadmindedness. All gods were given recognition and none was given real devotion, so that the educated classes drifted into an amiable religious indifference which soon degenerated into laxity of morals and eventually ended in a degradation of character which brought the ancient civilization to its death agony.

In the country, then, the church has lost prestige because of its narrowness, ignorance, and puritanical censoriousness. In the cities it has failed in influence because of its worldliness and indifference. The cultured congregation and its pastor lack spiritual power because nobody knows what they believe; the village or small-town minister and his people fail because they believe, or think they must declare their belief, in so many things that are not worth acceptance. No one who is not in constant contact with ministerial life can have the faintest idea how many good men in the ministry are eating out their hearts because they have tried to stem the tide of indifference or bigotry and feel that they have made no

progress. Nor can one who does not know from
the inside realize how many are slowly finding
themselves and securing firm standing ground midway between what Doctor Joseph Fort Newton
calls an arid liberalism and an acrid literalism. The
task of these interpreters of religion in terms of
modern thought is all the more difficult because
their battle is a lonely one. The multitude of sects
and the poverty of parishes have tempted church
authorities to accept and encourage an unedu-
cated ministry, poorly equipped to solve the problems of a new day; and the man who strives
must keep on without intellectual or moral comradeship with many of his fellows.

If this is, perhaps, the peculiar difficulty of the
small-town parson, the city clergy, on the other
hand, are handicapped by the lack of time for
concentrated thought. Many ministers are so over-
whelmed in parochial organizations that they have
little opportunity for reading, much less for digest-
ing what they have read. How many really strong
preachers can be found in New York to-day? More
often still, they are so entangled with those social elements which most deserve condemnation
that they lose fineness of spiritual fibre. In some
cases their entanglements are commercial, industrial, or economic, as well as social. The city parish is a huge financial enterprise; the men who
support it are identified with the world of indus-

try and finance, and it would be difficult to decide to how large an extent economic determinism may mould the thought, influence the preaching, and unconsciously regulate the practice of the spiritual leaders of large and important congregations. There are some of us, indeed, who suspect that " the activity of the clergy in every good work"—the energy with which they throw themselves into every movement of social and political reform, the readiness with which they are attached to new causes—is a symptom of their own restlessness and dissatisfaction, an effort to silence the call of a permanently troubled conscience; exactly as we suspect that many of the laity give way to a passion for moral reform as a refuge from "the tyranny of thought."

All of us, ministers and everybody, are living in a changing world, with new conditions developing daily, a world still war torn, witnessing new industrial developments, new national readjustments, clashing class interests. Those of us who are engaged in religious work feel the strain of this. And we have the added difficulty of adjusting our work to other conditions concomitant with these changes: the astounding growth of urban population, the development of apartment-house life, the breaking down of home influences and domestic traditions, the increase of comforts and luxuries, and the consequent removal of moral restraints and safeguards, the increasing opportunities for recreation. In the development of city life, with its quick changes in residential conditions, have come problems arising from shifting populations, the removal of those whose contributions for church work were most generous and disinterested, the stranding of once prosperous churches in down-town business districts or deteriorating residential sections, the equally tragic abandonment of village churches and the weakening of small-town parishes, and because of the loss of denominational enthusiasm—or, for that matter, church zeal and devotion—no corresponding increase of suburban growth. It is no unusual thing to hear the frank acknowledgment among church leaders that we must recognize the loss of one generation and prepare now to win the next. With the ackowledgment comes a ready recognition that the blame need not be placed upon the shoulders of churchmen of other days. They may have lacked vision, but so also was there lack of foresight in city planning, in community co-operation, in problems of government, in scores of other things wherein failure is now freely recognized and as freely excused.

IV

It is no wonder, then, that the church has lost prestige; no wonder, indeed, that for several decades the ministry has not been attracting the keenest minds. The hope lies in the fact that we are beginning to diagnose our disease. As soon as enough of us discover that we are really sick, there will be physicians to effect a cure, or, if you like to put it in the language of the preacher (which thing I abhor) there will be prophetic voices to recall us to our task with a renewed spirit. Such voices are already heard, and in most theological schools there has been steady improvement in the quality of the student body and in the spirit of the faculty membership. Some are wrestling bravely with the problems the ministry must solve in the new generation.

How, then, shall the church regain its prestige? Or, to put it in a better way, how may it become a stronger influence in the community, mould business and industrial life, improve social and political moralities? It is possible for the clergy to become a positive force in public affairs? Can their influence really be an active one unless they enter politics in championship of particular legislative proposals? Let us agree that their real duty is the inculcation of right principles, yet how can they actually accomplish anything if they are to enunciate general principles without specific application of these principles in legislative enactment, or social, industrial, economic, and moral reforms? The church, of course, cannot admit that moral questions of this sort are outside its province. Out of the disagreements and uncertainties as to how far the church should go, perhaps this fundamental statement may be accepted: Wherever a moral question arises, it is the function of the church to establish the principles upon which the question shall be determined. Beyond establishing principles the church generally should not go; but individual members of the church, acting in their capacity as citizens, often united in organizations, must see that right principles are duly expressed in specific reforms even though the exact line cannot be fixed between too much and too little reliance upon measures designed to carry moral principles into effect.

The point of divergence between this statement and the present trend of popular practice in the Protestant churches lies in the emphasis which it would put upon individual and associated action, rather than upon corporate action by the churches. An illustration in another field of moral endeavor may be taken from the educational world. Few men have exercised a more far-reaching influence in education than the beloved Dean Briggs of Harvard. He and his associates practically revolutionized the study of English. He "helped students to a right understanding of themselves, so that they could develop certain mental qualities of their own"; he "trained men to look at the world with their own eyes." Then the men who were so trained went into other educational institutions all over the country, carrying with them the ideas and methods they had learned and, in turn, the students they trained went away from other colleges by the thousands, taking with them the same ideas. The result is seen in methods which have created a new literature in America. In the same way, religious progress comes through the conversion and enlightenment of individuals and groups who become "keen centres of recovered consciousness of the church's true mission."

In the religious world Dean Hodges of Cambridge did a similar work. Week after week, year after year, he taught his students to judge moral problems with their own minds, meanwhile preaching the social gospel with homely effectiveness. These men in turn brought to the congregations in which they ministered a new sense of their social responsibility. Before he became dean of a theological school Doctor Hodges was a parish clergyman. He never identified himself with party movements; yet he quickened the consciences of his congregation to such an extent that an inefficient and corrupt local administration was turned out of office through their efforts—though, alas, the reform seems to have been only temporary.

Both men were chary of organization. Dean Briggs's strength lay in his intense interest in individuals, his real love of youth, his steady confidence in them, his ready trust in their essential goodness. Dean Hodges had the same confidence in human nature combined with a clear and unswerving faith in the social gospel which he taught. One transformed the spirit of the student body through his unremitting personal interest in individuals. The other was a powerful influence in transforming parochial life and making religion a saving power in the community for the redemption of society, rather than a spiritual medicine for individual use only. Difficult as it may be to put this into words, the distinction is quite clear between such methods and the enthusiasm of the Protestant ministers and churches of the present decade who prescribe how we shall live and how we shall think, what we shall put on and put off, what we shall eat and what we shall drink. It seems to have been the method of Jesus Christ himself, who always looked at life from above rather than from within, who did not issue his call to companies but addressed individuals, who never imposed an order of society but called men to a new way of life and so formed his kingdom by the conversion of men into subjects through their acceptance of The Way. He bids us now to make our lives a challenge and not a compromise and in fellowship with him to gain power to think clearly and act bravely. The minister must follow this method.

The present tendency is to minimize the pervasive influence of ideas and to rely upon legislation to effect reform. The temptation is to adopt the cruder methods of political propaganda and import into religious effort the commercialized methods of modern organization. The result is a reliance on regulatory codes which hardens its advocates into pharisaical self-righteousness and puritanical severity. Worse than that, the ministers and the churches become singularly obtuse to moral values and ready to excuse actions which in other circumstances would be frankly condemned. Witness the unconscious revelations of religious lobbyists who see no wrong in fighting fire with fire, are indifferent to the moral obliquity of paying public officials to become lecturers in advocacy of measures upon which they must vote as legislators, glory in their success at obtaining evidence by methods which shame the consciences of those who are not of the company of the saints, and can write the history of the prohibition movement as a clever political campagn, in complete obliviousness of the fact that it began as a moral revival and in this is its only possible excuse for continuance.

V

That brings us to another suggestion which may at first seem to be an anti-climax. To regain its prestige the church must return to the conviction that it exists as a spiritual centre of influence, a moral dynamic. Everything which weakens its spirituality lessens its real power. The protest against the up-and-coming methods of the day is not uttered merely as a plea for good taste or in disapproval of vulgar competition. Undoubtedly we need to get away from the stiff and starchy conventionalism of the past. The point is that these offenses against good taste destroy the spiritual appeal of the churches. Some one has said that Catholicism brings people to their knees in adoration, while Protestantism brings them to their feet in action. We need both. There must be service as well as sacrifice, work as well as worship. Yet it seems to many of us that the supreme need of to-day is a revival of the spirit of worship. The church which stands at the head of Wall Street, with open doors through which the distant altar may be seen, with groups of busy people entering for a few moments of prayer or silence, with services at convenient hours for busy people, with noon-day preaching of the simplest sort every day—such a church may mean more for the cause of real religion than a busy ecclesiastical organization whose minister spends his time with committees and clubs and in attendance upon outside organization and points with pride to a peppy basketball team, a live-wire Bible class, eager red, white, and blue committees engaged in Sabbath-school-attendance campaigns and all the complicated paraphernalia of community-house activity. Some of these things are good—in moderation—but the real need to-day is a recollection of the message of the prophet that in quietness and confidence is our strength. We live in a world of material progress. In America we have built up a great industrial and commercial system. Unless we can give it spiritual motivation it may become a huge Frankenstein monster suddenly endowed with power which we can no longer control, or a Juggernaut to grind us to powder.

So the church will regain influence as it regains spirituality. Its spiritual strength will increase as its clergy are freed from the activities which now leave them little time for thought or devotion. The clergy themselves must return to the realization of the duty to feed their own spirits, that they may in turn be a source of strength to others. One soul all on fire with real faith is worth more than a whole city aroused and curious. Faith like this will trust in something finer than disciplinary codes. It will have sufficient belief in humanity to feel that in moral decisions the individual may be left free to choose for himself. For a people who value democracy and have been taught to believe in the worth of the individual it will be clear that, while mass discipline, fixed rules, stern regulation may build up, for a time, a machine-like morality, in the long run that church will win respect which asks its people to decide for themselves, which even *compels* them to decide at the cost of honest mental and moral effort. Such a church will have a self-respecting constituency respected by others. It need never worry about its prestige. It need not implore an acknowledgment of its position. It will without such apologia find its authority recognized and its opinions and judgments carrying weight.

VI

Finally: The church will be restored to the confidence of the man outside when it gives more attention to the man outside. Too much effort is given now to coddling the "saints." When any effort is made at gaining others it is left to the crude work of spasmodic evangelism, and the churches confess their own weakness by combining in campaigns under the direction of imported experts in soul saving. Such efforts are as mistaken in their motives as they are offensive in method. They show no understanding of what Donald Hankey called "the religion of the inarticulate." God has many unattached followers, men of religious feelings and convictions who are not enrolled anywhere as Christian believers—often the very men whom we need inside the churches, men who are doing Christ's work and yet have not the stimulus of fellowship in Christ's church. That is our loss as well as theirs, and it is hard to say for which of us the loss is the more tragic. No effort can be successful which does not recognize this double loss.

Some things a ministry which is spiritually aroused will do; for it will necessarily be really interested in winning new disciples. It will be a studious ministry numbering men intensely interested in making Christian truth vital for the age. It must also be a teaching ministry, able to translate the truths of Christianity into terms of everyday life and express them, not in the language of dogma but in the language of the average man. Most churches have a cultural worship in highly developed form, or else free and easy evangelistic services devoid of reverence. Most sermons are either conventionally pious discourses or exasperating moral interpretations of current events, or half-baked social theorizing (a good bit of Bible slang; for "Ephraim was a cake not turned"), or fervid exhortations to sinners who usually are not there to hear the appeal. The average man has very simple ideas of religion. To him it means unselfishness, generosity, sincerity, cleanliness of soul, a genuineness and straightforward honesty that despises cant and is chary of religious professions, an abiding faith in goodness, a very real humility because of his own defects—which we are quite justified in calling penitence—a readiness, therefore, to forgive defects in others; with it all, a general consciousness of God, of whom he is rather vaguely aware though he finds it almost impossible to speak about Him easily and naturally. For such men there must be the simplest and most vivid preaching of the gospel story. We need clergymen the one passion of whose ministry will be to try to interpret the average man to himself and make him see that all the ideals of goodness he ever had are found in Jesus Christ. As for myself, I want to do more than that; I want to make men see that everything that Jesus Christ was God is. I want them to know that if there is a God he must be like Christ and I want them to believe that he is just that sort of a God in spite of all difficulties and in the face of all appearances to the contrary. I want them through Christ to be so certain of God that they will gladly give Him the undivided allegiance of their lives.

After all, that is what religion is. If we ministers are making this our task, we need never be ashamed of our calling. If men see that this is what we are trying to do, they will not long withhold their interest. If all the churches will make this their first aim, our miserable and inveterate divisions will be healed and the day of Christian unity will sooner dawn. This, indeed, is the real road to unity. When churches concentrate upon this common and essential service, denominational differences will fade: the weak will be united in strength; the common task will lead to common understanding; the Church will replace the churches. And the Church will be respected where churches are not.

SAVING SOULS THROUGH CHURCH SUPPERS

SAVING SOULS THROUGH CHURCH SUPPERS

I

Jim and I were returning from the monthly dinner of the Men's Club. I had been the speaker of the evening, and was now painfully conscious that the address had not been very inspiring, nor quite successful in its attempt to lift high the note of eloquence and make the stars in their courses take notice. Now came the sad aftermath of "staircase" wit—clever things forgotten and other brilliant things thought of too late. "Rotten performance, wasn't it?" said Jim, and I at once became apologetic: "Well, I wasn't up to the mark, but——"

"Now, now," interrupted my young friend, "I didn't mean your speech; I meant the whole darned thing. I have heard you in better form, to be sure, but of course there was no intended criticism of the evening's oratory; if the address had been so bad, I would be the last one to say so; I can occasionally shut my mouth like a clam. I'm just weary with men's clubs in general and this dinner in particular. Did you notice the crowd tonight? There must have been a hundred and fifty men present, and I'll wager half of them were there under compulsion. I'm a married man and a

vestryman. A sense of duty dragged me out, because the parson asked the vestry to show up. I
might have stifled the voice of a conscience which
is usually under reasonable control, but my wife
wouldn't let me forget. Well, to-night I looked at
the rest of the men, and I'll lay any amount that
a lot of them felt exactly as I was feeling. Why
should we drag ourselves away from home, on one
of our few free evenings, to eat a poor dinner, try
to talk to men we don't know, listen to an amateur
quartet, sing our own songs off key, and be afflicted
with the punk tenor we were obliged to applaud
to-night?

"Of course the parson wanted us there to do
the glad-hand act. Well, I'm no good at the job.
I'm not a 'good mixer.' I can't jolly people along,
and pull off a pretense of good-fellowship with a
lot of men of whom I haven't the slightest knowledge, who probably care no more about the stunt
than I do, who are about as much interested in
me personally as I am in them, and in most cases
would feel far more free and comfortable if I
stayed at home and let them alone. I went out of
a mistaken sense of duty. So did several dozen
other people. Some dozens more were driven there
by their wives or mothers. What good does it all
accomplish? We cut a good bridge party for this
church show. I can go out to dinner any evening.
If I want to hear music I can get something bet-

ter worth hearing in some of the concerts I've had
to dig up good coin to support. The Lord knows I
don't want to leave home and wife and mother to
sing 'Sweet Adeline' and the rest of the stuff we
had to-night."

I tried to make Jim see that the methods to
which he objected were evidence of the desire to
humanize religion. "It isn't just an endeavor to
save souls through church suppers," I said, "nor
is it a mild social movement to bring men together regardless of class or position. The fact is
that these dinners and smokers, and all that goes
with them, are signs of a change in religious ideas;
they are a reaction from the stiffness and starch-
iness which characterized church people of the
past; puritanism began to die when smoking and
even dancing and card-playing invaded the parish
house."

Jim couldn't see it. "Perhaps it started in some
such way," he said, "but a decade or two of that
sort of thing has destroyed its usefulness. For that
matter, would not the women, if they were honest,
acknowledge that they are just as bored by their
doings? Do you suppose they get much 'kick' out
of the Ladies' Aid meetings and the Missionary
Society? Do not most of them, like the men, go
because 'it's their duty'? Did you ever hear of any
one attending a church supper or a parish bazaar
voluntarily, in a spirit of exuberant or expectant

gladness? Do you imagine that, even in the Young People's Fellowship, pure joy is always unconfined?"

And then he added: "I'm serious about this thing. Why can't we go to church on Sunday without some usher to give us the glad hand, the Lord only knows how often, between the church door and the pew, especially if we turn up in the evening? What have all these social gatherings really done for the parish? As a matter of fact, aren't we simply spending our time refining enough oil to make the wheels go round? What does all the machinery make? Why in Heaven's name can't we have a religion that lets a man say his prayers in peace and then leaves him in the enjoyment of life, liberty, and the pursuit of happiness, without all this paraphernalia of pretended enjoyment? I've reached the point where I even hate to see the parson shaking hands."

II

The indignant protest of the bored vestryman touches on a problem of modern church work which is quite as acute as are some of the theological difficulties of religious life in these days of change, and perhaps more difficult of solution than many of the questions of policy or finance which seem to loom larger.

For, after all, friendly fellowship is vital to church life. According to biblical usage, the "saints" were not people who had attained to a marked degree of holiness, but those who had heard the "call to holiness"—church-members, in other words. "The communion of saints" meant, therefore, "the fellowship of the faithful." No church is really walking in the way of Christ which is not bringing its members together in friendly service, kindling brotherly understanding, promoting mutual confidence, breaking down social barriers, clearing away class prejudices, and spreading as by contagion the simple human spirit of Christianity. If the minister seems academic and impractical in his plans for making his parish a real "family in Christ," he is nevertheless bound to keep on trying. He himself is in the best possible position to be a mediating influence between head-workers and hand-workers, a bridge across the chasm which separates rich and poor. Not over-rich himself, and yet rarely falling below a decent poverty, he has an unusual opportunity to create a general social consciousness, and he is recreant to duty if he does not press on, however often he fails.

Moreover, never was there a time when there was such need as now to use every possible method for the creating of a parochial *esprit de corps.* Those whose memories run back three or four

decades know that then the congregation lived in
the immediate neighborhood, were likely to be
of the same social status, for the most part knew
each other more or less intimately in every-day
life, and in consequence did not feel special need
of the social activities which characterize modern
parish life. Now, especially in city churches, the
members of the congregation are widely scattered,
their parochial affiliation is more or less loosely
formed, their interest in the parish itself is not
sufficiently personal and individual to inspire to
active service, or even to help in creating a spirit
of corporate worship. Something must be done to
make each parish a social entity. Something is absolutely necessary if those who sit side by side at
worship are to be drawn together in common
work and provided with an outlet for the expression of that faith of which they receive impressions in the church itself. Services must issue in
service, and service usually needs to be corporate
and social.

My bored young friend had also forgotten that
his own circumstances were more fortunate than
those of the mass of his companions at the parish
dinner. He felt like the small boy trudging home
with his father under a load of approved pic-
nic paraphernalia and murmuring thoughtfully:
"Father, a holiday is lots harder work than just
every day, isn't it?" But it did not follow that all

the other men suffered from the same depression. Jim had friends with whom he might have been dining, or going to the theatre, or dancing, or playing cards; some of the other men at the dinner, however, were lonely young fellows recently come to the city, without acquaintances, much less friends. One is never quite as lonely as when he is a stranger in a crowd. Every city is full of strangers. Even in the smaller communities the lack of facilities for social enjoyment makes the parish house almost a necessity, especially in these days when we have become so accustomed to "being entertained" that the secret of self-entertainment has been lost, and the mass of people are without inner resources and cannot make provision for their own intellectual, recreational, and social needs. To some of the men whom Jim had watched that evening the dinner was a real event. At any rate, it is certain that if those who attended under compulsion or from a sense of duty had "let themselves go," in a real human way, and with the desire to get something as well as give something, the evening would not have been wholly wasted.

Meanwhile, in the parish house other meetings were in progress, day and night, bringing young men and women together—boys' clubs, girls' classes, gymnasium meetings, basketball games, brotherhood classes, women's societies, study classes, Girls' Friendly activities, ranging from classes in dancing to dressmaking and millinery instruction—even cooking classes, with promises of radiant satisfaction to delicatessen diners who know not home cooking and here, while looking in at the parish-house kitchens, might have found hope for days to come. The activities of the city parish house, well equipped from swimming-pool to dormitory, are beyond cataloguing. I call to mind one parish which lists fifty-six different organizations at work. Even in the smaller places, the women, in particular, find abundant opportunity for special service. Too often, it is true, they are merely hurrying to catch up with a threatening deficit, or working to pay old debts. Now and then it is suggested that the various social activities be abandoned, with all the labor involved, and the money raised by subscriptions from the harassed workers who (it is thought) would gladly pay to be relieved of their tasks; yet almost always it develops that the social enjoyments outweigh the disadvantages of the older methods, and the women pursue their accustomed ways with some small sense of satisfaction. Whatever may be the case in the large city, certainly this fairly represents the small-town reaction.

III

Nevertheless, even there, the practical questions will not down: How many people feel like Jim? How many of them are bored? How many come under compulsion, and so eventually cease to come? Do many of the others get much out of the system? Can we not find some better way of creating a family spirit, of rendering friendly service, of spreading the idea that individual fellowship must be kept strong and steady through corporate union, and that corporate union means even more than this safeguarding of individual attachment, that it must move out into the community and not merely hold the believer but save the world?

Laymen, as well as clergymen, must face these questions and give serious thought to the difficulties of church work under modern conditions. Grant that many attendants at parochial functions are present only out of loyalty, yet something in the way of social activity must go on, if members of congregations are to create a group-consciousness; and surely it is worth while to reach toward such warmth of cordiality in these days when a constantly shifting population needs parochial fellowship, when home life has lost much of its old-time appeal, when parish customs are not easily maintained, and parish loyalty is hard to create.

When Jim left me I tried to think things out, so far as men's dinners were concerned. They had, indeed, sometimes seemed to me only boresome functions animated by the Bostonian idea that baked beans were the manna which Heaven showered on the children of Israel. But—I attended many such gatherings and the guests came only once a month. They heard one speech, and I— Heaven pity me—had to listen to my own voice again and again before they arrived for their next rally. They were fortunate beings, invited solely to eat, drink (water or weak coffee), and be merry, at some other fellow's expense, while Jim was supposed to be a gifted being whose charm would shed radiance over the occasion, and I was a distinguished and unhappy orator working my passage. Perhaps Jim and I could not look at the spectacle save through jaundiced eyes.

I asked the rector about it. At first he was inclined to join in my questionings—poor man, he had a continuous round of such engagements himself. Once in a while, when extra notices grew numerous, he said he felt like passing it up to the choir. "They have been singing such meaningless and saccharine anthems of late," he said hesitatingly, "that I wonder whether it might not be good to have them relieve the minister by chanting the notices. Isn't that quite an idea? The congregation would certainly get some benefit from it. It would not take long to get up a whole hymn of notices, say to a familiar tune like 'St. Ann':

> "'The Young Men's Club will meet again
> On Thursday next at seven;
> Please bring a friend to dine with us,
> Lead some one else to heaven.'"

Yet on second thought he felt, despite our pessimism, that the thing was worth while, because it gave him and his people an opening for pastoral contacts which could be found in no other way. "In the city," he said, "the clergy face special problems because modern home conditions demand real pastoral effort, while at the same time effective care through pastoral calling is becoming increasingly difficult. Many a city clergyman spends a whole afternoon in calling, with no more satisfactory record at the close of the day than the counting of cards left at apartments where they may never be found by parishioners. What are we to do about it, unless we use these social occasions as opportunities for closer contacts with the men and women who are most in need of this friendly help and may find it a prelude to spiritual guidance?"

Even he, however, felt constrained to admit that we have passed beyond the period when the institutional church can be expected to meet the needs of the day, and that clubs, societies, parish-house activities no longer carry the same appeal, when (for so large a proportion of the church-membership) a dozen organizations supply what at one time the church was the means of securing, and the radio and other conveniences make many social activities no longer a necessity. The time has come when we must depend less upon parochial activity and more upon inspirational preaching, with all its severe intellectual and moral demands on the clergy; upon clear and definite teaching; most of all, upon a new emphasis on worship, with an earnest effort to make such worship truly congregational in character.

Of course there is a demand for stronger preaching. Sometimes one marvels, when the sermon is over, that so many people still go to church. It is true that much of the criticism of the pulpit is unjust. I myself listen to many speeches, as well as make many, and I cannot see that the average lawyer is a brilliant pleader, or the average after-dinner speaker or noonday-luncheon orator a shining success; but, making all allowances, it cannot be denied that the clergy do not, as a rule, think very clearly, or make their teaching as well as their preaching definite and effective. We cannot all be Fosdicks, but we can be clear, logical, definite, and informing;   certainly   the   sensation-mongering

preachers must soon discover, from the example
of Fosdick and others, that people are hungry for
sincerity and truth; that they are keener than
ever before in recognizing what is thin and superficial; that while an occasional vaudeville pulpit-
eer may attract a crowd, the permanent results
are perilously threatening to religion. If evidence
were needed to prove the degeneration of the pulpit, among men of the baser sort, I have a col-
lection of sermon subjects gathered from newspaper announcements in one section—of the East,
not of the Middle West. "Thanks for the Buggy
Ride" was one preacher's effort to pile sensation
upon sensation. "Syracuse to Hell and Return"
promised "spiritual interpretations" of a well-
remembered murder case. One man, returning from
his vacation, announced as the sermon-subject,
"Back Home Again and Dead Broke." It proved
to be only a sermon on the prodigal son. We may
only hope that the preacher made it perfectly
clear that he had not been feeding, at his summer
hotel, on "the husks that the swine did eat." "The
Tragedy of the Tuxedo" was but a mildly innocuous address about the guest who had not on a
wedding-garment. "They Satisfy" was one of a
series of sermons on advertising slogans, which
told of the comfort of divine grace; "Eventually,
Why Not Now?" had to do with the need of conversion; and "Three in One Oil" was the unthink-

ingly blasphemous effort of a pulpit Babbitt who preached on the Holy Trinity!

The decline of the pulpit may be due, in some measure, to the contagion of the parish house, with its hysterical effort to provide fresh entertainment through "live-wire" talks and "peppy" addresses. That sort of spiritual food will not satisfy a new generation which has turned away from religion and must be won back to Religion. Even "pulpit yawpers" will discover in time that the church must be more than a "Boosters' Club of Zenith City." Then men who know what they believe, and express their faith, simply and quietly, but with the forcefulness that always comes from real conviction, will find a hearing—and more than a hearing, a glad acceptance—by a parish group, in the minister's pastoral care, under his spiritual guidance, anxious to put into practice his teachings.

IV

At any rate, the definitely institutional parish has had its day, save in certain neighborhoods and to meet special demands. In New York one of the most famous parish houses has lately been demolished and a new and wholly different structure has been erected in its place, to meet new needs. St. George's and St. Bartholomew's, in New York, were pioneers in such institutional work. All over the country there was an effort to reproduce their work on a small scale, without their conditions, or their equipment, their trained workers—or even people on whom and with whom to work. Unquestionably the passion for such building had good results; despite comparative failures, men were trained to meet varied conditions, to know all classes of people, to understand social conditions, to be alert in emergencies.

Then came the social-service movement. Just as institutional churches led the way until communities took over most of the work they were doing, so the churches gave inspiration in social service, and to-day a great deal of the work which they sponsored has also become a community responsibility. There is a feeling now that organization is overdone. More and more parishes are learning to co-operate in community work. In one parish, in a moderate-sized city with which I am familiar, there are 400 of its members working in various community-welfare organizations, and working with the definite idea that their service in these societies is as distinctly "church" work as if it were done within the walls of the parish house; it is their individual "expression" of religion. Elsewhere a like story could be told.

Some questions are presenting themselves in this readjustment. What distinction, for example, shall we make between social service and Christian

social service? If it is the part of the State or city
to provide community recreational facilities, cor-
rective institutions, care of the unemployed, regulation of working-men's compensation, pensions
for mothers, insurance for old age and the like;
if professional social service is to undertake major
relief and deal with social maladjustments, what
is left for the churches? Is their work to cover
those activities which are based specifically on the
teachings of Christ as to individual and social responsibility? Has professional social service become so secularized that the church must do work
on similar lines, to conserve spiritual values? In
its anxiety to be non-sectarian, has it become non-
spiritual, concerned only with physical needs and
readjustments, and failing to do its part in co-
operating with those religious agencies which give
spiritual ministrations and seek to rehabilitate
the whole man? In its initial stage the social-welfare movement was officered, directed, and inspired
in large measure, by Christian workers who sought
to render distinctly Christian service. If it has
now become secularized, is it not the primary duty
of the churches to provide more Christian social
workers, rather than to create additional Christian social work? If so, must not distinctly parochial service seek a new outlet?

All these are questions whose answers affect
very intimately the social life of the parish house.

It must still be a centre of parish activities, and must still be used for those social contacts which develop a parish consciousness; but it will probably be a different kind of a workshop from what it was under old conditions. Study classes for special groups, small discussion classes, larger organizations such as the once popular public forum (which died when it became only a safety-valve to allow every variety of crank to blow off steam), young people's fellowships, with their serious purpose to enlist the enthusiasm of youth and train young people in organization and work, every sort of organization to interest busy people in the problems of religion and life—these will still make the parish house a hive of industry. Men's clubs will still give opportunity for fellowship, or at least there will be occasional men's meetings and men's dinners, but they will no longer begin and end in dishes and ashes; every men's club dies unless work is found for the men to do and a serious effort made to enlist their interest in real discussions of life problems and frank study of the difficulties of faith and morals. One of the newer parish houses in a great city has been built with the distinct aim of making it a cultural centre. The old parish house aimed at recreation and amusement in pleasant but not always purposeful ways; the new one will have an auditorium where "splendid young men and women, living on slender salaries, but eager and enthusiastic, may express their social impulses in an environment of kindred selves." The clergyman who planned it feels that here he can gather "young poets, musicians, artists, and dramatists who need only the opportunity to find themselves to bring out the rich resources of the world they live in." There will be a library, small class and lecture rooms, club quarters, adequate facilities for hospitality.

Such a parish house will be a home of friendship. It will be a gathering-place of youth, even offering daily kindergarten privileges at a modest fee to younger parents who respond to the ideals set forth. It will be a home of helpfulness, where character and personality may find expression for the sake of what they give and not merely for what they get. Boundless wealth has made it possible to give ideal quarters for this particular work, but it may give to smaller parishes the inspiration to do a like work in more modest surroundings. And just as the work among men and youth will slowly be revolutionized, so the very spirit of the parish will be changed. What form the readjustment in distinctly women's work will take in smaller churches is as yet uncertain; probably there will be combinations and larger cooperation, with parish councils giving direction. The church itself will more and more become a parish through such work methods, with parish

traditions, a distinct corporate life, its own special
character, its peculiar "atmosphere," and its inherited loyalties. Everywhere the clergy will be
seriously considering what changes must be made
in the type of worship offered, with new forms of
devotion tried out and new hours of service tested.
Noonday services, celebrations of Holy Communion at convenient hours, such as the popular Len-
ten services of the Episcopal Church (which others
are now trying out), and the noonday masses for
Roman Catholics during the same season; "children's corners"; the church school to take the
place of the old Sunday-school, with classrooms
and graded courses of study, with week-day religious instruction, with special services for the
young—these will remake the church as thoroughly as the new organization will remake parish
life.

V

And the thoughtful minister knows that his real
hope lies in the coming generation, whatever the
mothers in Israel may think of the manners and
morals of youth. He feels a special call to serve
youth, because he knows, as does no one else, how
tragically their interests have been overlooked by
the generation now passing. Because of this neglect
we find, among young people of high-school and
college age, an appalling ignorance of the simplest

facts of Christianity and of the fundamental truths
of the Christian life and its moral teaching. While,
however, their ignorance is often amazing, they
are really keen to know the truth. They have
broken with tradition; they will no longer accept
ideas on mere authority; they cannot and will not
blindly believe; but they can be equipped to do
their own thinking, guided and directed into real
thinking, led out of mere questionings into belief,
taught to distinguish between essentials and non-
essentials of faith, led to see what the Christian
faith actually is rather than left to reject certain
caricatures of it which they assume to be the real
thing.

Practically all of the Christian communions are
now turning in force to work among the youth in
our colleges, though quite conscious that they are
handicapped because of the neglect to prepare the
students earlier, before they came to college age.
We are doing what we can, with limited means, to
bring to these young people a true conception of
the Christian religion. The task is made surpass-
ingly difficult, because these thousands of students
come, at a most impressionable age, into the restless social and intellectual life of the college, freed
from some of the restraints which even yet are
credited to the home, starting on the adventure
of life with little or no preparation for its dangers
and temptations. Their naïve idea of Christianity

indicates a sad lack of pastoral care and teaching at home, and a still more sad lack of knowledge and training on the part of their parents. Therefore, while trying to lead these youth into straight thinking, the college pastors are crying aloud to the clergy at home to do the work among the youth there which will make easier the task of the college pastor in the coming years. The parish house of the future ought to be headquarters for such work. It will be, for youth and for those of riper age, a school of instruction in faith and practice as well as a social hall; it will train rather than amuse, educate for work as well as provide a meeting-place for workers. The "glad hand" will be less in evidence, though cordial fellowship will mark the effort to fill the open mind. There will be fewer "feeds" for the body and more "food" for the soul. The call to teach and teach and teach again, to think and think hard, will be clearly sounded, whatever other calls may be heard.

All denominational differences must, so far as consistent with conviction, sink into insignificance at this evangelistic call. I was talking recently with a railroad man who was somewhat wrathful because he had just come from a conference of the heads of the operating department of the road where, as he expressed it, the men had become so absorbed each in pushing some pet scheme of improvement that they forgot to look at their problems in the large. "Finally," he said, "I rose in my wrath and said to them: 'Gentlemen, you seem to think that the operating department is an organization for working new theories to perfection. Don't forget that our job is to carry freight and passengers. If we don't have them, your beautiful theories will sing to the winds.'"

There is in these words an obvious lesson for those who do the church's work.

CREEDS AND CHRISTIAN UNITY

CREEDS AND CHRISTIAN UNITY

I

CHURCH unity is in the air—in more senses than one. Sometimes it seems pretty far up in the air. Some of us feel that discussion of it will never get down to solid earth, until we endeavor to be more honest in our pleas and arguments. The Lausanne Conference on Faith and Order came perilously near to shipwreck, at the close, not because some plain-speaking delegates objected to the final report of the conference, but because, up to that point, everything had gone so smilingly that some of the more timid folk became hysterical when others ventured to suggest that the road to unity lay not through camouflaging differences but by bravely facing the fact of their existence.

The Lausanne Conference was never intended to bring about immediate reunion in miraculously short order. It was a gathering of friendly representatives of many churches, anxious each to understand the other. It was an Ecclesiastical League of Nations endeavoring to move toward peace, and realizing that the first step toward peace lay along the road of such mutual understanding. Its purpose was to give opportunity to each delegation to explain its own position, earnestly to seek to comprehend the view-point of others, and then to endeavor to frame a statement of fundamentals that would express common agreements, state frankly, but charitably, certain disagreements, and leave the reports as a basis for further study in an atmosphere of kindliness and charity such as the conference itself created, and might possibly carry to its constituent members. It would not have been a real help to such sympathy of consideration of the main problem, had vital differences of opinion been kept under cover.

In the same way, the Malines Conversations marked an effort at like friendly explanation on the part of Roman Catholics and Anglicans. The pronouncement of the Pope which synchronized with the publication of the Malines report was discouraging, not simply because of its flat declaration that the only road to union was the road to Rome; the disheartening thing was the fact that there was no attempt on the part of the papal advisers to accept, with any indication of graciousness, the basis of common understanding already reached, or to use this for complete explanation of the papal system, as well as because it seemed evident, also, that the pronouncement was timed to create the greatest possible embarrassment to the English participants.

And yet—did not the encyclical clear the air by its thunder? And may it not remind us that the fatal obstacle to real understanding among the churches which are seeking unity is a weak amiability which leads us to talk in dulcet tones and avoid the more courageous course of plain-speaking? May we not, all of us, be overgentle in agreements, soft of speech, while really inwardly aware of our own unyielding and inflexible attitudes? I suggest that this may be so, because I know that it is true of my own communion. I do not believe we shall make much progress, save as we endeavor to get down to realities.

Unquestionably, a chief characteristic of the American Episcopal Church is its unfailing amiability. Now amiability may be a beautiful virtue, or it may become a besetting sin. It may be the happy expression of one's kindly attitude toward life. For the most part Anglican Churchmen have never been narrow, aggressive, or disputatious. Modern Puritanism finds little in common with our ways. We do not stand at attention to pick quarrels with people who enjoy life in other fashion than our own ideas commend. We do not engage in violent agitation, nor are we fond of dictatorial methods of moral reform. We live and let live. We have never set forth a book of discipline. We have little love for personal piety based upon and backed up by legal enforcement. On the whole we are an agreeable and pleasant people to live with.

Our theological position also has usually been well balanced and kindly. We have never been harsh in our judgment of the beliefs of others. The Articles of Religion (called our "Forty Stripes Save One") were not a challenge of orthodoxy, but a more or less successful attempt at a comprehensiveness which would include without compromise of principle. Midway between Rome and Protestantism, we tried to set forth the truth in each system and to express the faith of the ages in terms that would hold within the Anglican communion sympathizers with both extremes of thought. Of course violently aggressive extremists refused to be satisfied with what seemed to them a compromise, but for the most part the Articles accomplished their purpose, and at any rate the Anglican Church was fairly successful in combining evangelical truth with catholic order. As a matter of fact, we have usually lived on amiable terms with both Rome and Dissent, even at the expense of considerable internal discomforts of our own. Our theology, our practice, our discipline have made for peace.

But amiability has its perils. It may be so sweet as to be cloying. I, for example, may be so mildly propitiatory as to cause grave suspicion of my moral earnestness. Liberality toward men of other minds *may* indicate an absence of deep conviction. Kindliness in matters of discipline—as any one

could testify who knows much about the internal
affairs of the average diocese—may mean simply
that we haven't as much backbone as a chocolate
eclair. Amiability may manifest itself in flabby indifference in faith, with a harmlessly negative and
conventional code of morals; a halting and apologetic substitute for vital religion, a stodgy and
stolid mediocrity, unconscious of its failures because unambitious in its spiritual ideals; without
earnestness of purpose, without enthusiasm, without serious anxiety to be of worth in the Kingdom, without militant and aggressive adventure
for Christ.

II

The amiability of Anglicanism is nowhere more
manifest than in our attitude toward church unity.
The whole movement of the present day received
its impulse from us. We naturally dislike the sectarian spirit. Our own liberality in what we deem
non-essentials has made us impatient of the narrowness of denominationalism. Moreover, our
neighborly attitude toward Protestantism has
made us conscious of the weakness and ineffective-
ness of disunion, while at the same time our ideal
of comprehensiveness has enabled us to grasp a
catholic conception of the church. We believe in
one holy, catholic church; and the clergy, at least,

put loyalty to the whole church above partisan zeal for our own branch of the church.

For a time our desire for unity led us to reach out hopefully toward Rome—and we were repulsed. Then we made eyes toward the East, though apparently no one except ourselves knew we were trying to flirt with the Mistress of Orthodoxy. Now we are extending friendly hands toward Protestantism, and for all our friendliness but succeed in being seriously misunderstood. Yet, however often we may be ignored, repelled or misunderstood, there is something in the genius of Anglican catholicity that makes it impossible to give up the effort toward unity. Because we put loyalty to the catholic ideal above belief in our particular branch of the church, we naturally desire unity as the expression of the ideal. We can never be content till the family of Christ has caught again the family spirit, settled its differences and come together in peace and unity, with mutual understanding, mutual concessions if need be, mutual love and appreciation and singleness of purpose and effort. A less amiable folk would cease following what some regard as a will o' the wisp. A more aggressive people would be content to proselyte and spread its own propaganda rather than urge co-operation. Our liberality forbids such a course. Our amiability is a virtue.

But is it also a vice—a weakness, a sin, a curse?

Chesterton, who says many a true word in such humorous and startling fashion that he seems but to jest, tells us that we talk too much about "respecting" this or that person's religion, forgetting that the way to respect a religion is to treat it as a religion; that is, to ask what are its tenets and what are the consequences of such tenets. "Historians," he says, "seem to have forgotten two facts—first, that men act from ideas; and second, that it might therefore be well to discover *which ideas*." It is an amiable weakness and a fatal error not to know or care about the creed from which a people's customs, good or bad, will necessarily flow.

And he also reminds us that this sentimental kindliness only irritates people who have real convictions. "We are always saying to a Mormon or a Moslem, 'Never mind about your religion; come to my arms'; to which he naturally replies, 'But I do mind about my religion and I advise you to mind your eye.'" He has an amusing story of a militant Christian and a blatant Atheist who became firm friends because, amid a world of indifferent folk, they discovered that they alone were in dead earnest about the things they accepted or rejected.

We Anglicans, in an endeavor to satisfy widely divergent theological views, have often been amiable to the point of ambiguity and obscurity. Some one has said that the "Reformation Settlement" was really a thing which left many things unsettled, a sort of "gentlemen's agreement" that if possible they were to be left permanently undetermined. There was some virtue in this. It was a characteristically English way of progress through compromise. But it may be questioned whether the general moral effect upon Anglicanism has not been to make us dangerously expert in balancing on the fence. Enthusiasm, one way or the other, is apt to be with us a lost art. We have developed a spirit of languid tolerance which plays with great realities and will neither assert nor deny. Our religion, too often, expends itself in the effort to live on terms of peace with everybody. We sometimes forget that to have the fierce sun of truth beat hot upon the black shadow of doubt is better than to live in a universal mist which makes the world a blur and befogs our moral perceptions.

Sometimes one feels that we are allowing our besetting sin to beguile us into a pleasing self-deception in the matter of Christian unity. It takes a little courage to say this, because one is apt to be misunderstood. Moreover, where the underlying purpose is so worthy, one dislikes to be critical or contentious.

III

The demand for unity has become insistent. Back of the demand lie many motives. The "man in the street" gives the movement tolerant approval because he is impatient of "dogmas that divide." Hard-headed laymen back it for practical and economic reasons. Advocates of social and industrial reform are interested because they look toward a united church as the only agency through which moral impulses can be given to a new social order. More and more the clergy long for it because they see the weakness of a divided Christendom, unable constantly to speak the truth, boldly to rebuke vice, patiently to suffer, if need be, for the truth's sake, and bravely to bear witness for Christ; the futility of an army even of friendly allies without a united command, its inability to win the war for righteousness or hold for Christ a field already won. At its best the demand for unity is a real hunger of the heart, a passionate desire of men of many minds but of one spirit —the spirit of Christ their Master.

But is it not true, then, that the stronger our desire for unity becomes and the deeper our motive, the more anxious we should be lest a false unity deceive our hopes? It will not do, in this of all things, to allow ourselves to be dazzled by glittering generalities or soothed into content by sentimental aspirations. Because we want the thing so hard we want to make sure that it is the real thing we are offered. Therefore, before we can consider the means toward unity or the terms on which it is to be based, we need to make sure of our conception of unity itself. It will be fatal to refuse to face facts; tragically ludicrous if we deceive ourselves by amiable sentimentality.

A church unity mainly bent on politely ignoring differences and calling one another by kindly names would be similarly charged with centrifugal impulses. It would fly to pieces as rapidly as it was patched together. There are fundamentals in religion on which churches may unite, because the fundamental principles of religion go deeper than the political principles of democracy. There are non-essentials on which we may agree to disagree, because we put loyalty to Christ above all party or sectarian spirit. Just now, our difficulty is, that we seem to be afraid to declare what we consider fundamental and anxious to sentimentalize into ambiguity all serious differences. Before we can accomplish much in preparing the way for unity, we must agree upon our goal. Before we discuss any basis of union for the church we must discover what we believe in common about the church. It is foolish and futile to seek for unity save as first we are willing courageously to face

primary considerations, without which real unity
is unattainable and the amalgamation which we
substitute for it would contain so many discord-
ant elements that it would quickly fly apart again
into a multiplicity of fragments.

We want church unity. Well, first, then, are we
agreed on the need of a church? Is the very idea
of a corporate Christianity the forethought of
Christ or merely the afterthought of men? At the
preliminary conference in Geneva, on Faith and
Order, Bishop Gore pressed this point strongly
and with the courage of consecrated sincerity and
conviction. "I want to know," he said, "whether
we cannot go back to the beginning and ask ourselves what really is in the mind of Christ and
what really were the intentions of his first interpreters with regard to the unity of the church. I
want to know whether we can start afresh and
whether we can in any way agree as to what we
mean by the church and by the unity of the
church. Do we find an obligatory membership in
a visible society to be the characteristic of Christianity? In the New Testament I do not seem to
find anything which is entitled to call itself membership of Christ which is not also membership of
this one visible body."

Such considerations as these, it seems to me, we
are bound to press home to ourselves. Behind any
movement for Christian unity must lie the ques-

tion: Are we actually agreed that the name of
Jesus is the only name under Heaven whereby
men may be saved? Are we agreed that his earthly
life is truly the unveiling of Deity? Before we go
on to church unity, we must face the question: Are
we actually agreed that a visible church is really
necessary and that membership in it is of obligation? Before we can logically talk about any ar-
rangements for ordination in the united church,
we must ask: Are we actually agreed that any sort
of a divinely commissioned ministry was really
established for the continuance cf the faith? Never
mind, for the present, whether it be a priestly
ministry or not; is any ministry actually necessary
or could we get on without such an arm of the
church? A little uncomfortably, perhaps, at first,
but rather gladly after we had learned modern
methods of work. And the sacraments: Are we
actually agreed even on a simple basis of belief
about them? Are they means of grace ordained by
Christ? or beautiful ceremonies sanctioned by
Him? or ancient rites dating from later days and
evolved out of other religions? Why talk longer
about a united church, if we are not agreed in the
first place on the necessity of a church? If the
church be nothing more than a convenience—on
the whole a very satisfactory method of securing
unity of Christian purpose—then there is no actual compelling motive for becoming a church

member, and the question of uniting all these conveniently useful societies into a common order becomes for me wholly academic—or shall I say, economic? I cannot, for the life of me, get up any enthusiasm about it; or more than a very little interest.

IV

Do such considerations bring the whole matter of unity to an absolute *impasse?* I think not. The truth is, they do not change the situation in any degree; they merely compel us to face facts. We have been shutting our eyes in amiable dread lest we should see unpleasant differences; we have politely refused to believe that there are any obstacles. The cause of unity will not be aided by such self-deception. The surest way to advance it is by bravely recognizing facts and honestly meeting conditions. The need of unity has never been felt so strongly as now; the desire for it has never been so keen; the movement has never before developed on such spiritual lines. All this creates an atmosphere in which we may better consider our convictions. The longing for unity has now become a real hunger of the heart for faith. It has brought us to penitence for past errors and mistakes. It can bring us to shame and regret for past prejudices and misunderstandings. There could not be better conditions for the consideration of primary convictions. Too often, in the past, theological discussions have been a matching of wits. Mind has met mind in intellectual debate. Now heart may meet heart in penitent effort toward mutual understanding.

This is all the more necessary because we cannot think of the church that is to be as a sort of highest common factor of all the sects. It is to be a splendid combination of all the finest qualities of Christian faith that are now displayed in separation. It will hold truths in due balance as conviction is matched by conviction, and as realities, felt all too strongly by some because wholly unappreciated by others, are now set in place against other realities in a rounded completeness of faith, worship, and practice. All this means that our real task is to make others understand the things we hold essential while we seek to appreciate the things which to them are equally valuable. Instead, a false charity has impelled us politely to assure each other that all of us are very much alike and that nothing really matters. For myself, I am convinced that the road to unity is not a mere line of least resistance. Unity will not be made effective by casting convictions into the discard; rather will it come when convictions are frankly discussed, constructively not controversially.

We have grown in fuller appreciation of some

of the treasures others have guarded. Despite what has been said above, I believe many of us in the church have really come to think of unity less as a compromise for the sake of peace and more as a comprehension for the sake of truth. For this reason I believe the time has come when we should honestly and bravely seek to explain ourselves and out of our differences reach toward the unity which will synthesize contraries and apparent contradictions and so reach a wholeness of truth by combining the positive teaching that lies back of every denial.

The church, of course, does not exist for the purpose of formulating creeds and proclaiming dogmas. Moreover, the church's duty is not merely to teach the faith; but so to teach it that it may frame and fashion the lives of her children. The creed is more than creed. It is at once creed and character, dogma and devotion, logic and life. Nor is faith mere intellectual assent to credal formularies; it is receptivity of soul; it is the consent of the whole man—mind, conscience, heart, will— to the will of God as revealed in Jesus Christ. When, therefore, we urge some fundamental agreement of faith as a prerequisite to unity, we do not ask for agreement as an intellectual covenant or even as an intellectual basis for action. Rather, we consider such an agreement on essentials to be necessary because, with Chesterton, we believe ideas

control conduct. Our whole thought of the meaning and purpose of life depends upon our grasp
of spiritual realities. False or imperfect doctrines
will and must result in lives faulty and maimed,
which might have been complete.

The end of faith and worship is life. If this is so,
the full Christian creed is vitally necessary. Its
presentation should be as simple as possible, re-
duced to real essentials, but in these essential elements it must be consistently presented and fully
preserved, because out of it springs the Christian
character. The ideal life which we call the Christian life sprang out of the faith which we call the
Christian faith. As Scott Holland says: "We cannot unravel the threads which knit the character
which we know in its developed form as Christian,
from the creed which appears, at every single point
of the character, as its inherent and vital background." I do not believe that it is possible to
drop out of the law of Christ its theological value
and yet retain its ethical value. With Scott Holland again, I believe that the sickness of the hour
has resulted from the attempt to abstract the
creed of the church from the ethical ideal of the
church. "Men are sick and miserable and weak as
soon as their thought has no definite relation to
their moral practice. The absurd and ignorant assumption that Christianity is a separate matter
from its dogmatic belief persuades men to accept

a false division, which attempts to break up the undivided unity of the man, to sever the inseparable. No wonder they find themselves enfeebled and ensnared by an impossible divorce."

Finally, I say as strongly as it is possible to say it, that in any doctrinal basis for reunion, we must be overcareful to distinguish between essentials and non-essentials. In the interpretation of truth as in the expression of devotion, there must always be accommodation to temperament and taste. Even that will be possible, if we can work back to the core of Christian faith. Is it hopeless to expect that? I do not think so. But I do think that in order to secure such a basis of agreement, we must all have something more far-reaching and radical. We all of us need something of conversion if we are to see visions and appreciate ideals. We need to return to God.

THE GLORY OF THE CHRISTIAN FAITH

THE GLORY OF THE CHRISTIAN FAITH

I

PERHAPS I am not as puzzled, nor even as penitent, as some of my confessions would indicate. Certainly I am not so puzzled as to have any doubts as to where my stand is to be taken on the foundation facts of the Christian faith and life.

This seems to be a day of uncertainties and of countless varieties of belief and practice. In my own church a few excited persons, banded together for "church defense," have been making the welkin ring with their demands for the expulsion of some of the brethren whom they suspect of being enamoured of Rome. On the other hand, they themselves are under suspicion by the opponents; first, of being lawbreakers themselves in their absolute disregard of the church's discipline; second, as being none too sound in the faith.

On this latter point, particularly, the laity are puzzled. They cannot understand, nor can I, how in all honesty any clergyman can read the prayers of the church and lead his congregation in the recital of its creeds, if he cannot say those creeds without equivocation or mental reservation. They cannot understand, nor can I, the type of mind so lacking in plain common sense that it replies to

the charge of dishonesty by declaring that all who
do not believe that Christ is sitting on a gold
throne above the bright blue sky are guilty of a
like insincerity, in proclaiming that "He ascended
into heaven and sitteth on the right hand of the
Father." They cannot understand, nor can I, how
any one can fail to see the difference between
language that is plainly full of figure and symbol,
and other language that cannot be regarded as
merely figurative without the utter loss of all
sense and meaning. They cannot understand, nor
can I, how any man can declare in the chancel
that he believes in Jesus Christ, God's only Son,
our Lord, who was conceived by the Holy Ghost
and born of the Virgin Mary, and then fifteen
minutes later attack those who say that the language has a plain and simple meaning which no
dialectics can possibly pervert. They cannot understand, nor can I, how clergymen who have no call
whatever to deliver a spiritual message unless first
they feel in their hearts that it has been delivered
to them as ambassadors of God, can waste precious moments of worship in crude denunciations
of beliefs or opinions that they have not taken the
trouble to study carefully. They cannot understand, nor can I, how any one can be willing to
distress devout souls by negations, when men's
hearts are hungry for positive guidance in matters
of faith and practice. The ordinary layman regards

the clergyman's office as one of dignity and importance, and he cannot understand, nor can I, the irreverent and casual temper of mind that will turn the pulpit into an intemperate forum of abuse, denunciation, and denial.

What I can understand, though many of the laymen cannot, is that it is not possible summarily to turn out of the ministry any man whose mental perversity permits him to do these things. I can readily realize that no bishop should have such arbitrary power as would permit him, even with the counsel and advice of others, to take immediate and drastic action against every offender. The priest has rights as well as the bishop or the layman, and such rights must be safeguarded. I know also that a heresy trial would be fraught with more evil and danger than would inaction. It is better to tread the path of patient endurance than to toss into the market-place for discussion the most sacred beliefs of religion. It is wiser to wait for error eventually to correct itself than to let loose the passions, give opportunity for the intrigues and risk the misunderstandings that have accompanied every heresy trial of former generations.

II

Our chief need at present is to think calmly and clearly, and try to keep the real issue unconfused.

The question must not be clouded. Unless those who have talked with me are extraordinarily far from being typical of the mass of people, there can be no doubt that these questions are not clear to many. Some seem to think that the issue is drawn between the Modernist and the so-called Fundamentalist, and that unless we accept the radical views of the most "advanced" school of modern theologians, we are forced to accept the extreme of intransigence. Many questions have been injected into the problem which do not belong there at all. Those who defend the faith need not, by any manner of means, be believers in the literal verbal inspiration of the Scriptures; they are not obliged to discard belief in the wonderful revelation which has come to us through the prophets simply because they have come to see that the Bible was not dictated word by word and syllable by syllable from God's lips. There is a reasonable belief in inspiration which sees that it is in no way inconsistent with the use of human instrumentalities, with all their human characteristics, varieties of temperament, imperfection of temper, differences of fundamental conceptions, of breadth of vision, direction of outlook, tendency to error. The wonderful thing about the Old Testament is that with all its imperfections it gives us the record of a nation's developing faith in God—a faith which grew and held firm despite the annihilation of the

nation in which it had its birth. The worship of
surrounding nations long since ceased to hold its
followers. An image is a wooden thing; it cannot
grow. Israel's idea of God was a living conception,
constantly developing.

Nor is the real question one of biblical interpretation. The man who declares that orthodoxy insists upon a prosaic and literal interpretation of
the creation stories of Genesis is simply tilting
against windmills. The biblical account is a great
creation poem. The Bible is not an inspired man-
ual of science nor a divinely dictated hand-book
of history. It is a guide-book to faith. It is the
record of an evolution in the idea of God. The
various steps in the development of the conception of God are so unique and extraordinary that
we believe they are due to revelation from the divine personality. The one thing unique about human personality is that it cannot be confined; it is
always outflowing, always self-revealing. Character is always being communicated. We believe that
in God there is that which is the divine counter-
part of our own personality, and so we are ready
to believe that this "super" personality is also
outflowing and self-revealing.

Again, the issue is not one of any particular
theory about miracles. The real religious difficulty
of to-day lies in the fact that many people have an
inherent prejudice against the possibility of mira-

cles, because (consciously or unconsciously) they have been influenced by modern science and its idea of the reign of law. We must try to get rid of this prejudice. To say that God rules the world of nature by law does not mean that he created the universe and then left it to run by itself. To believe in the reign of law does, indeed, involve a change of belief in what we call "miracles," but it need not force us to complete disbelief. We are merely reminded that there are laws of God's operation which we have not yet discovered.

Once more, the real issue in all discussions of the miraculous birth of Christ, or of his bodily resurrection, need not be condensed into any phrase about his exercise of the power of God. Grant that he was divine, yet he submitted to certain human limitations when he entered into human life, and only so much of the power of his divine personality was exercised as is perfectly consistent with a true human existence and development. He "emptied himself" of his divine privilege when he took upon himself the form of a servant and was made in the likeness of men. He exercised the powers of deity, but we believe he could do so because his perfect and sinless humanity was wholly responsive to the power of God.

So we have cleared away the ground. Some one has cleverly observed that the phrases which have been thrown about in the discussions of the past

few years have been harmless epithets to frighten
the unwary. Like the naughty boy who jumps out
from behind the door and shouts "Boo" at his un-
suspecting sister, so (to quote a recent sermon)
certain mischievous controversialists have been
shouting sounding words to frighten timid souls
who have not yet discovered what all the confusion
means and therefore fear the worst.

III

What, then, is the real issue before us? It is this:
Have we, or have we not, an authoritative revelation of God in Jesus Christ? We have no such revelation unless his life is actually the unveiling of
deity.

It was a wonderful thing that Jesus Christ did
for religion—nothing less than the rediscovery of
God. We cannot read the New Testament without finding the wonder and surprise of that discovery on almost every page. Religion in Christ's
day had become formal, conventional, fixed and
hard. The Hebrew regarded himself and his nation
as the special favorites of God. God had indeed
made Israel his chosen people; but he had not
chosen them out of favoritism nor to confer upon
them a privilege to be selfishly grasped. He had
chosen them that they might be his instruments
and agents in bringing the knowledge of himself

to the world. They hugged their privilege to their own breasts. Pride in their calling made them hard and unsympathetic toward all who could not conform to their requirements. Even those who were faithful in their performance of the routine of worship lost its spirit. Are there not similar conditions to-day? God is lost now, as he was then, "in the maze of religious machinery."

And God was indeed lost then—wholly misunderstood. The Hebrews made him even such an one as themselves. God had become a sort of Magnified Man sitting in the centre of the universe, ruling things and judging people. There grew up a religion which made it more important to observe rules and keep feasts and fasts and follow customs and conform to ceremonies than to love and serve. God became cold, distant, unapproachable.

Then Jesus Christ brought God back to men. Religion became fresh, real, wonderful, beautiful. God became near, human, friendly, approachable. A thrill came again into religion. Worship became devotion to a person. Service became the glad labor of those who were fellow workers with God. The God of Jesus was Friend and Father; a friend to be known, remembered, honored, and into whose likeness men grow through companionship and intercourse; a father who cares for his children and will do all that a father can to win them to love and loyalty; a father who comes forth to meet his returning children with forgiveness and pardon; one who goes out to seek and to save as a shepherd seeks the wandering sheep on the mountainside. In other words, God is like Christ; like him as he walked with his disciples through the fields and hills of Galilee; like him as he talked with them in the intimacy of daily life and slept with them under the stars; like Christ in his devotion to truth and right, no matter what it cost or in what it ended; like Christ as he led his friends in the path of duty; like him as he sacrificed and suffered, that they might know and care; like him in his gentleness and goodness, but like him in his hatred of sin as well as in his love of sinners; like Christ in his presence and power—not the power of force which compels, but the power of love that wins and attracts.

God is like Christ. That is the essence of Christianity. It is not enough to say that Christ is Godlike; no, God is Christlike. "The heart of God is as the heart of Jesus." That is our standing ground amid all the changes of time. That is our faith, though all things on earth shriek denial against it. That is the heart's assurance amid life's dark mysteries, when trials beset and sorrows befall us. That is our constant belief when wars ravage the earth, when social injustice ruins the souls of the poor, when the heavens are as brass and the earth totters under our feet.

God is like Christ. It is what he himself said when he declared that those who had seen him had seen the Father—and whoever recorded the words, they have in them the ring of truth. God is like Christ. That is what St. Paul meant when he spoke of the light of the knowledge of the glory of God in the face of Jésus Christ. That is what another writer meant, when he spoke of the God who in other times was made known through the prophets, but was now revealed in his Son, the effulgence of the Father's glory and the very stamped copy of his substance. That is what St. John meant when he said that the life was manifested and that he had seen it and was bearing witness and was showing unto men that eternal life which was with the Father and had not been manifested. "That which we have seen and heard," he writes, "that which our eyes have looked upon and our hands have handled of the Word of Life, declare we unto you." There is in the very words, as I repeat them, a gladness of surprise, a reverent astonishment, a breathless devotion, an awe and wonder that hush and still us. The God of Jesus is the only God we can really believe in. If God is not what Christ said he was, he ought to be—we can never again be content with anything less. Christ let men read down deep into his heart and then told them that God was just like himself. He called on men to follow him, to live his life, to

think his thoughts after him, to test by the beauty
and glory they saw in him every idea of God they
had ever had, and to find in him truth and life.

IV

How comes it, then, that men have minimized
this central truth of the Christian religion? Because, just as Israel had pushed God far away, so
Christian teachers, in proclaiming Christ's deity,
made him remote and unapproachable. Because,
just as the Hebrews had mistaken their calling, so
Christian theologians became hardened to a dogmatic task and in the attempt to define Christ in
exactly the right words, forgot sometimes to follow the God whom he revealed, with reverence
and humble sincerity. Because of the hard and
dogmatic way in which the truth was taught.
There are two ways of teaching doctrine. It may
be taught as a revelation leading to life, giving to
life value and rich abundance; or it may be made
a shibboleth to shut out all who cannot frame
their lips to pronounce a test word aright. Doctrine may be concentrated into tabloids of truth,
pestilent little pellets offered for spiritual health
but thrust down one's throat if not voluntarily
accepted—perhaps, therefore, bitter to the taste
and repellent to the recipient.

Moreover, the fact of Christ's deity was emphasized at the expense of his humanity. The Christian faith is the treasure-box of the riches of God. When I go to a safety-vault to unlock my deposit-box I need two keys. When we would unlock the treasure-box of God's truth, we need the key of Christ's divinity, but we need also the key of his humanity. The faith of Christianity declares that Christ is not only perfectly God, but completely Man. He entered into human life to translate the thought of God into human language and the life of God into a human example.

Men are essentially single-tracked in their road to thought. They usually see only one truth at a time. Theologians, keen on preserving the truth of Christ's divinity, minimized his humanity. So there came the cry which was the characteristic note of the passing generation, "Back to Jesus"; back from creeds and councils, back from dogmas and conciliar decrees, back to the Jesus who lived among men.

> Behold Him now where He comes,
>   Not the Christ of our subtle creeds
> But the Christ of our hearts and homes,
>   Our hopes and prayers and needs,
> The brother of want and blame,
>   The lover of women and men,
> With a love that puts to shame
>   All passions of mortal ken.

We needed to be recalled to this truth. The church has again and again been recalled to it. The singular fact is, that the real battle of the church has always been the struggle to maintain the reality of Christ's humanity. In the early councils it was never as hard to define his deity as to safeguard the completeness of his humanity. Yet it was done successfully, without diminution of his godhead, and it must be done now.

We needed, I repeat, to be recalled to the truth of Christ's human life and example. The preaching and teaching of this truth have been very real and very moving. The life of Christ, as it has been pictured for us of recent years, has indeed a haunting beauty; it casts a spell upon the mind; it hushes the heart. We see Christ as we never saw him before, in relation to the world's life and the world's need. We appreciate much in his words that had been forgotten. We find in his example inspiration that had been almost lost. The thought of his cross as the greatest act of heroism and self-sacrifice in history has made the world know him, not simply as "Jesus, meek and gentle," but as the "strong Son of God." We know now that he never came to make life easy; he came to make men strong and great.

Yes, it was needed, and it is all very beautiful. But it is not enough. We can never build a real and vital faith on only a human Christ. We must see the value of Christ's teaching, realize the worth and wonder of his example, know his solution of life's problems, see the power of his human faith and love to set in order a confused and distressed world; but we need more. Unless his voice is the voice of God, how can we know that his system will ever work? His teaching may be very beautiful, his life very wonderful, his thought of God very moving; but how can we be sure that he is not a dreamer whose dreams can never come true? Unless we have the conviction that his voice is the voice of God for us, his leadership can never be a sure leadership for all ages.

More than that. What is our greatest need, the real hunger of our hearts? Is it not to know what God is like and be sure? If Christ is only a man, what does he know of God more than the rest of mankind? His thought of God is high and splendid because he was the best and noblest of men; but he may have been mistaken. Indeed, apart from the resurrection, which declared him to be the Son of God with power, was not his life built upon a mistaken theory, and therefore bound to end in failure? His faith would not stand the strain of contact with a rough world. He tried it out and it proved to be a mistake—a glorious mistake, but a tragic one in its ending; a dream—a dream of beauty and splendor, but an impossible dream, notwithstanding.

No; it is one thing to have wonderful teaching

about God; but it is another thing to have a Christ who speaks, and has a right to speak, with the authority of God. If his voice is not God's voice, it cannot come to us with assurance. If his cross is but the world's worst tragedy, instead of God's adventure for a lost race, the spring of hope is gone from our hearts. If his proffered forgiveness and help are not by God's authority, we have heard but a swan song of gracious kindliness from a visionary lover of mankind. If those who have seen him have not seen the Father, then nobody knows what God is like and nobody ever will know. I cannot see any stopping-place between faith in Christ's divinity and blank agnosticism. All this, of course, is no proof of what the church proclaims. But neither is it a mere threatening gesture of protest. It is the solemn truth, expressed in a dilemma: Christ, or nothing; the certainty of God as Jesus proclaimed the Father, or blank uncertainty. I don't want any God but the God of Jesus Christ, nor do you; and if we cannot be sure that our Lord spake, we are all at sea again in our thought of God, and I can find across the barren waste of waters no course to a safe harbor.

V

What, then, is the road by which we come to our faith in the essential deity of Christ? By the same road along which the apostles reached their faith. They lived long enough with Christ and close enough to him to discover at last the secret of his personality. It seems to me that in one of Bishop Gore's latest books, *Belief in Christ,* we have one of the finest pieces of Christian Apologetics in all Anglican theology. He gives us a very vivid picture of the life of the apostles with their Master, and shows how the wonder of their experience grew until Christ came to have for them "all the values of God." They do not appear, at first, he says, to have asked themselves questions about Christ's person, and you cannot imagine his breaking in abruptly with any statement of his godhead; but he came to hold in their lives and in their minds that place which is the place of God only. He even claimed to be the ultimate and infallible judge of their lives. He declared that God had given to him the right to judge men, that men might honor him as they honored God. "He deliberately trained the disciples to trust in him utterly. For a man to put himself toward any other human soul in the very place of God would be supreme presumption, the sin of all sins, and yet that is exactly what Christ did of set purpose. He led the disciples so to believe on him as that they must discover him to be either God or one usurping God's place. He made upon them an impression of unbounded authority and power which absorbed their souls." Is it any wonder that gradually they came to see that he was all that he asserted himself to be? Their belief in him, but half formed at his death, was confirmed in his resurrection, through which he was seen as Lord of life and victor over the grave, and was "declared to be the Son of God with power." In other words, the disciples came to believe in Christ's Godhead through their experience of his human life. Coming so to believe, they passed on their faith as an inheritance to the Christian church, an inheritance which the perpetual experience of Christ's power in those who believe has made continually more credible.

This faith of the apostles was simple and unquestioning. It remained for St. Paul to give it form and expression as that became necessary, as of course soon happened; but when St. Paul set forth the truth on which they were already acting it was received without question. It is indeed the same fully developed faith as that of the Gospel which we call St. John's.

It is this faith which we find expressed in the creeds of the church—and by creeds, I mean the general statements of belief found in the so-called Apostles' Creed and the Nicene Creed, not the more modern "confessions of faith."

A study of the great councils of the church will show that creeds are but the careful expression of the facts of Christian experience. The doctrines of

Christianity are the logical exponents of its facts. We somehow have the idea (even the most thoughtful of us) that to regard creeds as of real importance is narrowly dogmatic, and to urge acceptance of them brings into religion the spirit of the drill sergeant. On the contrary, as Doctor Fosdick once reminded us, every statement of the creeds is the expression of a tremendous spiritual experience, and we need to be on our guard lest we reject any credal expression before trying to make the experience out of which it grew our own.

So the doctrinal decrees of the councils came to be adopted, not as one would build a fence to shut out unbelievers, but because belief both in the complete deity and in the real humanity of Christ had to be preserved if faith in him were to be retained. When Arius denied the true deity of Christ, making him less than God and more than man, the Christian society would really have relapsed into paganism had this teaching prevailed, for Christ would have been but one more demigod among an already extended list. When Nestorius became confused and declared that the Babe of Bethlehem was born a human person, Jesus, who afterward became controlled by the God, Christ, Christianity would have meant nothing had not his error been discovered and rejected. The very purpose of Christ's coming is to lift humanity into the life divine. The deification of one man could never have meant this, any more than had other so-called apotheoses.

Every error of every council has its parallel in our own time, and the clergyman who has not given thought to the problems the councils decided can never be a safe guide to his people in the intellectual difficulties of the present day. Take, for example, the question of the virgin birth of Christ, about which there is frequent doubt and difficulty. Of course, faith in Christ's deity does not rest upon faith in his virgin birth. On the contrary, we believe in the virgin birth because we believe in Christ. If we have definitely made up our minds as to Christ's divinity, then we know that his entrance into human life was something without equal or likeness in the annals of earth. The fact of Jesus himself is so unique and miraculous—the standing, continuous miracle of his life and character is so wonder-compelling—that we may rightly expect the method of his entrance into human life also to be unique. Indeed, if we are sure that the personality of Christ is the eternal personality of the Son of God, I do not see how we can possibly imagine his birth of a human father. A study of the council which considered the Nestorian doctrine would be a revelation to those who think there is anything new under the sun, especially any new error!

Young men come to me now, even as candidates

for the ministry, with the dimmest sort of knowledge of what they believe or why. Leaving homes where they have been taught nothing about God, they go to colleges where they must face, unprepared, the problems of faith. If they come through with any real religion, it is at best vague and colorless. Despite these spiritual handicaps, some feel the desire to serve and to be of use to their fellow men. They offer themselves for the ministry, with high purpose but with small knowledge. The true priest of God must do more than minister as a sort of glorified Y. M. C. A. secretary. He cannot do real social service even, unless through the power of the Holy Spirit. He cannot save men unless he can bring God to their hearts, and he cannot possibly make God real for any one else unless he knows God himself.

We think, some of us, I presume, that a right faith is of no special importance. There could be no more disastrous error. I have no doubt whatever in my own mind that the chief cause of the moral laxity of modern life runs back into indefiniteness of belief. It cannot be questioned, I think, that in general (that is, taking people in the large) the way in which men behave depends on their attitude toward spiritual verities. If they have, in general, no definite belief as to the meaning and purpose of life, men are bound to lower their moral standards. If there can be found no real authority in the teaching of Christ, it will have less hold on men than it has now—and God knows that is little enough. If we have no certainty as to what God is, or what he does, we shall have small incentive to serve him. If Christ may be regarded only as a human teacher, we shall have strange interpretations of his teaching—stranger even than some we have already.

CHRISTIAN LOYALTY AND CHURCH
LIBERALITY

CHRISTIAN LOYALTY AND CHURCH LIBERALITY

I

THE opening chapters of this book have had a more serious purpose than the criticism of certain unpleasant aspects of Christian enthusiasm. I have had in mind something vastly more important than laughing out of court the advocates of various nostrums for the welfare of the social order. I have been endeavoring to call the Christian churches of America back to what I believe to be our real task, the reforming and renewing of society by the winsomeness and attractiveness of the life and teaching of Jesus Christ. The church has a social mission and a social obligation; it must proclaim corporate righteousness and public morality, not merely call men to private and individual consecration of life. It seems to me, however, equally clear that while the church's voice should be heard as a directive influence in public morals, there is a great danger of our forgetting the distinction between moral teaching and the particular methods by which the moral teaching may be applied to problems of our complex life. It is a distinction, I have said, which is difficult to make clear in connection with the church's duty to-day; yet it is a real distinction. Some things the Christian denominations of America are doing which they never should have attempted, and the result has been too great a reliance upon legislation and the civil arm for the enforcement of morality.

I write, not by way of criticism, but in an effort to make it clear that, after all, the greatest possible contribution to any social or religious or political movement is the contribution of regenerated personalities. One by one, amid a distracting maze of programmes and panaceas for the reform of the world, men must be made to see that the real need is the reform of themselves. Jesus Christ was not, in the strict sense of the word, a reformer, certainly he was not a political reformer. He set forth no laws and regulations, framed no legislation, established no new social or industrial systems. He did something better: he inculcated a new spirit, set men in a new attitude toward one another, put a new leaven into all social life and relationships.

We need to ask, first, what the Christian religion is, and what it demands of us. I should like to show, also, if I may, the way in which the Episcopal Church presents the gospel; its sane and restrained methods; its gracious liberality and sympathetic understanding: I love it, as I compare its methods with others that are distasteful and even repellant. I want others to realize that it has such a spirit, because it has deep roots in the past.

Let us begin, then, with a simple statement of what Christianity is, and then go on to an understanding of how the church declares it.

The essence of the Christian faith is its authoritative revelation of God in Christ. The central truth—the very core of the Christian faith—is the assurance that "the heart of God is as the heart of Jesus." Jesus Christ is the Word of God, the perfect revelation of the thought of God, the translation into human form of the life of God. We need the assurance of this fact. Once we have the assurance, we feel something of the thrill that came to men with this rediscovery of God, as the apostles went forth to tell of it in words that even now seem trembling with emotion, words that hush us into silence as we read again of how these early disciples came to see "the light of the knowledge of the glory of God in the face of Jesus Christ."

II

That is but the beginning of the story. When one attempts to sum up the Gospel faith, one sees that, first of all, it tells us of a world in sin and in need of salvation. If we take time to think, do we not discover within ourselves the seeds of moral disaster? Sin is more than "an unfortunate slip, a foolish mistake, or a grave misfortune." Any man who takes stock of himself knows that sin is a deep-rooted moral disorder due to the deliberate setting of the human will against the will of God.

And then the Gospel tells us of a Saviour who came to give himself in sacrifice for the world's sin. However difficult it may be to understand the process of salvation, at least we can see that it would be impossible in this day to believe in any God save one who could enter into the world's tragedy and sorrow. We who have lived through a generation when millions of lives have been given in sacrifice that civilization might live, we who have sometimes since so despaired of that civilization as to doubt whether it deserves to live, surely we can see that atonement and sacrificial love are all of a piece with our own experience. We cannot understand how a God of love can make suffering a necessary condition of human existence or a medium of blessing; nor can we see why knowledge, civilization, health are purchased only by severe labor for us by others—in other words, through mediation—but, seeing that it is a universal law, we may dimly understand the necessity of Christ's atoning sacrifice, believe in it, and acquiesce in it as in harmony with God's law of love.

Sin is serious. Sacrificial love alone can cure it. And then, next, the Gospel tells us of a God who is not merely kind and benevolent, a loose, lax, easy-going deity who shuts his eyes to evil, but rather a God of majesty, of severity, and righteous indignation. We need to remember this, in a generation which is amazingly careless of moral standards and indifferent to moral obligations.

Once more, this Gospel tells us of a future life. If anything on earth is beyond controversy it is that the disciples of the Lord believed with all their hearts that Jesus Christ rose from the dead. They were as sure of it as they were of their own existence. And they were just as sure that his resurrection was a pledge of their own. Therein lay the wonder of their message. It satisfied the one great longing of the human heart, the desire to know of a surety whether there is another life, and whether those we have loved long since and lost are lost only for awhile. Christ not only made assurance doubly sure by his own victory, but he also filled men's hearts with trust in a heavenly Father, he so made them understand the real values of human life, that they came to take for granted that death is a mere turn in the road that leads to immortality. God being what he is, and man being God's child, it could not be otherwise. Any belief in immortality must rest back upon God's moral character, and Christ made that plain.

Nor was this all of his Gospel. He never meant

men to dream of another world while forgetful of the present world. And so he gave us a standard of human life splendid in service and sacrifice. Can we imagine any character finer and truer than his, as he takes the field in behalf of every threatened virtue, never swerving a hair's breadth in allegiance, never failing in affection, utterly unselfish, never weak, but brave, strong, and large-hearted, walking the way of truth and right, though it led to Calvary and the cross?

Finally, his Gospel tells us to sink self, as he did, in serving others, and promises that if we will start on this road there is abundance of grace in store for us to strengthen us on the way. Do we know of any course that will bring surer happiness?

III

Few of us are trying seriously and earnestly, in this way, to understand the glory of our faith. During the past winter I made a bit of an experiment in preaching. I have given, in various places, not sermons, but simple, vivid accounts of the four gospels. I have taken each of them and told their story simply as a story. I have, for example, told the story of St. John's Gospel and tried to make my congregations understand how it must have sounded when first heard as the record of one man's faith. I have not preached about it. I have simply painted a picture and trusted that those who looked at it would understand. I tried to show the growth of an apostle's faith from the day he first met the Christ until that evening in the upper chamber when the last doubting disciple fell on his knees at the Lord's feet with his cry of faith: "My Lord and my God."

It has been a wonderful experience to see how men and women listened, how they seemed to see as for the first time what the story really meant. And I have been quite sure that they felt the thrill of it almost as a new discovery. Alas! I have also felt that it came as fresh truth simply because they were making no real effort to learn the story for themselves. They do not read the Bible, with its record of the gradual revelation of God. They do not even read the four gospels, with their story of the God-Man, Jesus Christ. They are as pagan in their ignorance as those to whom we send missionaries in foreign parts. Read once more the story of our faith. Read it as little children. Put aside, for the moment, any questions about miracles, any difficulties of interpretation, and read until at least you have a working knowledge of the facts. And I promise you that the beauty and the wonder of it will reach your hearts and make faith easier. You will find something and it will be a treasure you would not let the wealth of the world buy away.

A missionary in India tells of a discussion he had with an able Hindu judge. "Well, after all," said the Hindu, "there is not much difference between us. You Christians are converted when you find God in Christ; we Hindus are converted when we find God in ourselves." "With this difference," said the missionary, "that in those countries where Christ is known you do meet men with whom as you talk you gather just this impression, that of light and discovery and inspiration, whereas I do not know of a single Hindu student who gives me the impression that he has found." The judge's face fell as he acknowledged the fact. "No," he said, "I do not know one who has found."

The real trouble with American Christians today is that they do not give this impression of discovery. They are active, some of them, in good works; they are generous in public benefactions; but they are so immersed in the materials of life that they have not found the real thing in life.

So I summon you to the search. Suppose we cease settling affairs of State, just for a few months, put aside what many of our leaders consider our duty toward world peace, international relations, industrial problems, and all the rest, and ask whether we have not been trying to build up Christian character and a Christian civilization with little foundation on which to build. Take for granted that people in our sect-torn denominationalism have not really been taught the first principles of the doctrine of Christ, and begin to teach them as new-born babes. That is what men need. Of this they are largely ignorant because we have not taught them. The eagerness with which they have reached for popular books on the life of Christ is evidence of a real hunger for faith.

Studdert Kennedy tells of a school boy who remarked to his master: "I cannot see the necessity for all this teaching about religion and social problems and all the rest. What use is it to us? We want to know how to behave ourselves in decent society, among cultured people, and maintain our position in life." And there are many among us with no larger conception of Christianity than that—men and women, conscious indeed that all society is not cultured and most of it far from decent, and rather proud of being at least above the average standard, who are content with this conventionally religious paganism and have never knelt at the feet of that stupendous and awful mystery, the King in his beauty, have never offered up the ancient sacrifice of a humble and contrite heart and have never, as Studdert Kennedy puts it, "felt the wonder of our own infinite littleness and of Christ's infinite greatness, stabbing at our vitals like a knife."

Let me put to you some questions partly in another's words: Do you think, or do you not think, that Christianity is played out? Does it really have your vote? Would you will it to be true? And about Jesus Christ himself—is he the nearest to God whom you've ever known or heard of? Would you rather have him as your God than any one else in the Day of Judgment—if Day of Judgment there is to be? Would you like your children to grow up as real Christians, or would you prefer to warn them against all that I have been writing, as an old superstition? Is it God's fault, or is it our fault, that Jesus Christ is now remote from our lives? When we do try to follow him, are we better, or are we worse? And how can we ever hope to follow, if we trust to the conflicting interpretations of him which a myriad host of teachers offer? Why not try to find out for ourselves what he is really like?

IV

Christianity is Christ—the Christ whose coming in the flesh was the unveiling of the heart of deity, whose life reveals God as Christlike in his love, whose teaching explains for us the mysteries of life, whose ministry ennobled human service, and whose moral standards for men and nations are the goal of all human endeavor. Whatever we know of God, we know through him. Whatever of good there is in modern civilization we owe to his teaching. Whatever of human helpfulness glorifies a life too often sordid and self-seeking is a reflection on his ministry of service. Whatever of help we need, he still stands ready to give. Whenever we fail, despite his help, it is of him and through him that we must seek forgiveness. Whatever of hope there is for the future lies in him—for at last men the world over are beginning to talk in strange ways of acceptance of the Christian spirit as the only saving power in a world that has been full of discord and confusion. If we would know how to live, we must go to him. If we would find strength to follow our knowledge, again we must go to him. If we need forgiveness for failure, he alone offers it.

He offers it through his church. We must make men feel the wonder of our Lord's life and the beauty of his teaching and give him devoted personal allegiance. A study of the gospels, however, will show that religion must not stop there. Christ never meant his followers to be left loose and unattached. He founded a church where individual fellowship might be safeguarded and kept strong and steady through corporate fellowship and service.

And so I plead for a clearer understanding of the need of church membership, worship, and service. There is a picture of Jesus Christ which has abiding beauty. It is a picture which shows him amid crowds of the poor who come to him for help and comfort, distressed and heavy laden who crowd

about him to obtain release, sick folk pressing
upon him to be healed, and he receiving them all
tenderly and graciously, giving generously, teaching simply and beautifully, till men are drawn to
him and long to be like him. The picture shows
him also as the Great Leader, strong, courageous,
unafraid, whose teaching had dynamic influence,
whose thoughts of truth and right have gradually
revolutionized our moral standards, supplanted
ancient tyrannies, and established human freedom
and equality of opportunity in every nation which
has genuinely accepted his Gospel.

Because he is such a Master, one sometimes
feels that the attempt to organize his followers
and to build up for them a system of teaching and
a regulated life, is to rob the Gospel of its sim-
plicity and take away its charm. That is not true.
You cannot read the story carefully without discovering in the mind of Christ another purpose,
a motive revealed at first only to the inner circle
of his disciples and to them but gradually. As the
years of his ministry draw to a close, he goes away
from the crowd, apparently puts aside opportunities of service, withdraws more and more into
privacy, is alone as much as possible with a small
group of friends, takes time to train them with
infinitely painstaking care, bends all his energies
toward making them understand the secret of his
life, and finally declares that upon the rock of their

faith he means to build his church. That was the real purpose of his life. Not simply to do the little good that could be done in those brief years, in one small corner of the world, but to train a band of men who would understand who and what he was, what his sacrifice means, and how his life was to be imparted to others, and would organize a church as the society through which his life would be made known, his death pleaded, and his teaching perpetuated—a church which would be more than a voluntary society, an organism in which his life was to be conveyed through sacramental channels.

That is the conception of Christ's eternal purpose which we need to lay hold upon in these days, when the idea has gone abroad that church membership is a matter of indifference or that even should we become members we may make our own church, if we will; the idea that the church is an "amorphous aggregation of individual souls," a society through which "a set of views may be promulgated"—and a more or less incoherent and unstable set of views, at that. I believe more than that. To me, the church is the Body of Christ, and Christianity is necessarily a life to be lived in corporate fellowship, its members having direct relation to the living Head of the Church and through him fellowship with each other.

V

It is because this is my belief about the church, that I am impatient of the attitude of certain types of Christian believers who lower the ideal. I cónfess that the sort of sermons I have heard of late are almost unendurable. I have grown weary of the thing for which the ministers of America seem to stand. They are altogether too sure about the sinfulness of the rest of us, and entirely too ready to regulate our lives for us. I want to regulate my own life. And I am glad to belong to a church where I am allowed to regulate it.

It seems to me that, despite our reputation for narrowness, the Episcopal Church is the most liberal of all Christian churches. By that I do not mean the false liberality which so enamours the modern mind. Chesterton (as already quoted elsewhere) reminds us that in the days of the Roman Empire the world once nearly died of broad-mindedness. All gods were given equal recognition and none was given real devotion. The educated world drifted into an amiable indifference about religious belief that soon degenerated into laxity of morals and eventually ended in a degradation of character that brought the ancient civilization to its death agony. We are in danger to-day of mistaking a similar false liberality for real breadth. The

Episcopal Church has true liberality. Sensitive to the influences of the Reformation period, it has yet, as Canon Carnegie says, maintained its institutional continuity with the past and along with it many of the usages and traditions of pre-Reformation catholicity. It has combined evangelical truth and catholic order and brought them together into some measure of mutual accommodation. It has made a splendid effort, and in large measure a successful effort, to combine Catholicity and Protestantism as complementary rather than contradictory forces. Many of us believe that if Christendom is ever to be united it will be through the agency of the Anglican communion.

Again: we have reason, at this particular time, to be proud of the liberality of the Episcopal Church in the matter of practical morality. American Protestantism has embraced a regulatory code of morals that shows only too many evidences of hardening into pharisaical self-righteousness. It has been altogether too ready to use the civil authority not only for the regulation of morals, but even for the standardization of thought. In pursuance of this regulatory policy, some of the Protestant churches have engaged in practices quite as objectionable as those of the professional politician. They have exerted political pressure in ways for which, in other days, they have condemned the Roman Church in unmeasured terms.

They seem to me to be launched upon a course which is as certain to bring disaster upon them as similar disaster followed upon the intrigues of Rome in the past. Their representatives have out-heroded Herod in the practice of the precept they once condemned in the Jesuits, that the end justifies the means.

I am proud to feel that for the most part the Episcopal Church has shown a real liberality of thought in such days of moral compulsion. We have always avoided disciplinary codes and regulations. We have felt that in moral decisions the individual should be left free. It has not been easy, always, to stand firmly on such a platform. Mass discipline, fixed rules, stern moral regulation—these have an apparent strength, just as Prussianism once seemed to make for national efficiency and Papalism for ecclesiastical concord. But for a people who value democracy and have been taught to believe in the worth of the individual, our own method of training the conscience must win, in the long run. You can build up a machinelike morality by disciplinary codes, but only through personal responsibility and the development of the individual conscience can you fix morality upon a sure foundation. Therefore I am proud of a church which leaves me to decide for myself what is right—which even *compels* me to decide, at the cost of honest mental effort—

and which does not tyrannize over my conscience and endeavor to standardize my brain.

And then I am proud of a church which realizes that its task is to call men to worship. Of course worship must be combined with service. We need work as well as worship. Yet it seems to me the supreme need to-day is the need the Episcopal Church emphasizes. We live in a world of marvellous material progress. In America we have built up a great industrial and commercial system. Unless we can give to it some spiritual motivation, it may develop into dangerous and destructive power. So the church sounds the call to worship, to the remembrance of God, to thought of spiritual realities. And it brings us to our knees in a service so dignified and impressive, so beautiful in form, and so inspiring in action, if made an act of congregational and corporate worship, that there is nothing of which I know, in any Christian body, to compare with it.

What puzzles me is that more people do not feel all this as I do. What puzzles me most is that Episcopalians themselves are often so dead to it all. There is a story of the late Father Stanton, of St. Alban's, Holbourn, which makes clear my meaning. Many still remember him as the most popular London preacher of his day, a man of personal magnetism and of somewhat spectacular methods such as frequently shocked conventional Englishmen. Once he entered the pulpit at St. Alban's, stood for a moment in silence, and then suddenly flung out his arms and shouted three times: "Fire! Fire! Fire!" Before the agitated congregation became panic-stricken he added quietly: "Everywhere, except in the hearts of you stolid English Church people." I do not know that he really awakened many of the congregation then present, but assuredly in time he converted and convinced thousands of others. I wish we could aid in this work of conversion.

A BISHOP LOOKS AT THE CHURCH

A BISHOP LOOKS AT THE CHURCH

I

ONE of my favorite stories, hoary with age but still a favorite because it happens to be true, tells of a genial clergyman named Taylor, who loved to travel in mufti and, while thus fairly well disguised, talk with the men he met in the smoking compartment. He had been joining in the conversation of a group who were all travelling men, giving their views on business and matching experiences in salesmanship. A remark by the clergyman led some one to ask for what firm he was travelling, and he replied, "For Lord and Taylor," and promptly relapsed into silence, without explaining his little joke. No one knew but that he, too, was a travelling man.

And, indeed, he was a member of a class who are always travelling. It is a little more than twelve years since I became a bishop. My diocese numbers a hundred and twenty-four ministers on its clergy rolls. When I made up my new list this year, I saw that more than two-thirds have come into the diocese in the past twelve years. Only thirty-four of the names on the list are of men who were here when I came, and of these thirteen are the names of retired clergy. Of the other twenty-one, only eleven are in the same parishes in which they were serving when my episcopate began; the others are still in the diocese, but they are in charge of other work than that in which they were placed a dozen years ago. There are one hundred and fifty-six churches and chapels in the diocese. Only one out of every fourteen is served by the same minister who was in charge twelve years ago. A like condition obtains elsewhere; other dioceses are no more stable than mine; in some the changes are even more numerous and conditions are more discouraging.

Nor does it appear that these conditions are peculiar to the Episcopal Church. In some Protestant denominations the changes of pastorates are much more frequent. These facts are not recorded in a spirit of self-satisfaction. I am not rejoicing in the comparison, as when a visitor in a certain village, which had four churches and adequately supported none, asked a pillar of one congregation, "How is your church getting on now?" and received the reply: "Not very well; but thank the Lord, the others are not doing any better."

With some of the Protestant ministers this restlessness is appalling for a further reason. Last year I had interviews with some thirty-six or thirty-seven ministers who consulted me about reception into the communion and priesthood of the Episcopal Church. For one reason or another they

were not only anxious to leave their parishes, but
desired to change their church affiliation. A few—
a very few—of these and others who have come to
me could be received. For the most part they would
never have fitted into a new environment, and it
would have been tragic to encourage them to try.
But the stories they told let in some light on the
general problem I was studying. Why did they
want to change? A few showed real change of convictions. Some came because they felt that Protestantism is disintegrating; that it is suffering
from the lack of a central administrative over-
sight; that it has no recognized source of authority; that there are no definite credal requirements and no acknowledged discipline. Others desired such a central authority, with episcopal over-
sight, because they felt they were at the mercy of
their congregations and were not free to preach the
whole truth as they saw it. Some even looked long-
ingly to Rome and, had they been unmarried,
might possibly have fled from the lay popes who,
they said, ruled over them to the tender mercies
of an Italian prelacy. Some were seriously searching for a better way; they felt the loss of reverence
in the methods of modern Protestantism; they
were attracted by the sacramental teaching of the
Roman Church and the Episcopal communion;
they were men of devotion who hoped to make
reality of worship the keynote of their ministry.

Most of them were weary of the nervous strain of competition—with the sermon exalted to the place of first importance, they found it impossible to run a race with the pulpit Babbitts who flourished all about them. Not a few, alas, were misfits and failures in their present positions, yet fondly convinced that their condition would improve elsewhere.

As I have said, we were obliged to discourage most of the applicants. They were too old to change. They were too "set" to make readjustments. They were too optimistic about conditions in the new church of their choice. They were fearful when told plainly of our own internal discomforts. Had they been encouraged to change, some of them would have felt that they had jumped out of the frying-pan into the fire. It was an adventure into the absurd to picture what might happen to those who would have "gone to Rome" —to let the imagination play on their experiences when they tried to submit to the regimentation of thought and practice that would have been necessary, once they had taken this step into the great unknown.

But they were all pathetic. Those who were misfits could not see that they were in any way at fault. The men who were considering a change too late to make it successfully were often tragic in their distress. In almost every case they were sure,

they said, of their call to the ministry. They had
entered upon it hopefully and enthusiastically.
But they had travelled "farther from the East,"
and though for a time by "the vision splendid"
they had been on their way attended, at last they
were perceiving it "die away and fade into the
light of common day."

II

Convinced, as I am, that the tales these men
told are evidence of a sad disintegration of American Protestantism, the conviction is accompanied
by no pharisaic impulse to thank God that I am not
as other men are. For in my own church the evidence of the clergy rolls prove that all is not well
in our Israel. There is little inclination, among
the clergy of the Episcopal Church, to change
their ecclesiastical affiliation. The much-heralded
transition of an occasional pervert to Rome is the
exception, not the rule. And for one of the clergy
of the Episcopal Church to give up his priesthood
for a more Protestant ministry is almost unheard
of. But the list of those who decide to return to
secular life, and ask to be deprived of their ministerial functions at the heavy price (almost disgrace) of an open renunciation of the ministry, is
quite appalling. Only the bishops realize how many
such cases there are, and only the bishops know

the heartaches that lie behind the record. I have been told by some in authority in the Roman Church that in spite of their *esprit de corps* restlessness, dissatisfaction, and occasional rebellion are on the increase, and that the tragedies would more often come to a head, were it not for the inherited tendency toward submission and the acceptance of a disciplinary system which at the same time allows for much flexibility in the transfer of men, not only to new work, but to new kinds of work where they may more readily adapt themselves to conditions and find peace and satisfaction in congenial service.

Much as we may dislike the very idea of Prussianism,—regimentation, over-submissive obedience to authority, standardization of thought, unquestioned acceptance of regulations,—we know that in the ecclesiastical system, as in government, autocracy does work at times. There are many in my own church who wish to have a larger power of mission conferred upon the bishops. They forget that the Roman rule works with a celibate clergy who may easily be moved about, whereas it would not work so smoothly when wives and families must be moved with them. They forget also that too large a measure of authority usually leads to abuse. Even the Methodist Episcopal Church (whose bishops, in this respect at any rate, are bishops indeed!) has found, on occasion, that

authority can become harsh. Methodist ministers
are not always happy. Rome is Rome. In church,
as in civil, government, the rest of us are endeavoring to work out our salvation as a democracy, convinced that in the long run democracy
will outwear autocracy. Even for the sake of
smoothness in operation we are not willing to give
up our freedom of initiative and independence of
action. Much less are we willing to admit, despite
its failures, that the ideal of a married ministry,
living the normal life in close contact with the
congregation, is not an ideal sweet and true and
beautiful and worth sacrifices to maintain.

And so the minister travels. On and on he and
his family move, ever hoping for happier conditions, ever being disappointed. Even if the minister were to stay, our problem would not be
solved. For, if he does not change, the congregation does. Once he could remain a score of years
in one parish, ministering to the same parishioners
and to their children after them; now his congregation is a rapidly moving procession. They come
and go. In the villages and small towns many of
the ablest and most progressive and adventurous
of their people move to the cities. In the cities
they move from apartment to apartment, never
abiding long enough to convert steam radiators
into hearthstones. There, too, success often means
a longer move to a larger city and a more impor-

tant position, until abundant success carries the happy traveller to Baltimore, to Philadelphia, Boston, Chicago, or to the Glorious Babylon of the New World, whence the only move to a higher place comes with death—and one is not quite certain that even this will mean for some a translation to the Blessed Isles.

III

Moving America, which has lost almost all conception of the meaning of the word home, may in part account for a moving ministry. But the explanation leaves much still to be explained. Why are the clergy not only restless, but discontented, sometimes miserably unhappy, often hopelessly fallen from their early enthusiasms?

One of the most effective sermons I ever preached owed its success to an accidental piece of good psychology. It was in no way an extraordinary bit of homiletical persuasiveness, but the congregation liked it, and I was fortunate in having one keen listener explain why. It was a sermon on reality in religion, designed to show that Christ is impatient—divinely impatient—of anything that savors in the least of mere careless and conventional acceptance of his teaching, or a nonchalant belief in himself. In his presence we must be perfectly honest with ourselves and perfectly straightforward and unaffected; he despises cant. I had a great deal to say about downright sincerity among Christian people, but by good fortune I said none of this until I had first made public acknowledgment of certain clerical shortcomings. I pictured the man outside the church who stayed outside because of a certain smug professionalism in some of the clergy which irritated and annoyed him. I confessed that our immunity from friendly criticism had been disastrous. I acknowledged that our words do not always ring true; we find it only too easy to drop into a habit of ready moralizing that is wholly perfunctory and smacks of pious cant. My friend told me that the congregation recognized the picture and gladly acclaimed the facts as to my confessed sins. "Having won them to complete accord in your portrayal of clerical faults," he said, "their innate good sportsmanship made it impossible for them to deny their own sins when you pointed them out. It was good psychology to begin with yourself."

And so it may not be unkind to look for the faults in the clergy themselves, if we are to find the full explanation of their restless dissatisfaction. Indeed, it may not be amiss to begin with bishops; and herein are included not only bishops like myself, but the "higher clergy" of all denominations—presiding elders, archdeacons, heads of ecclesiastical departments, bureaucrats in general.

Perhaps we might be more sympathetic and helpful to the clergy, if we had some one to criticise us; but we too are immune,—that is, from face-to-face criticism. Many people talk about our faults and failings, but always behind our backs; we have few friends who are courageous enough to talk to us plainly, as man to man. In consequence we are apt to "put on side" and become impatient of disagreement with our plans or policies. We do not hear much about our blunders, and usually succeed in keeping our own eyes shut to their consequences. A bishop gets a large idea of his own attractive powers, because he is usually greeted by a splendid congregation and sees a church at its best. He is credited with unusual preaching ability, because some one hears a sermon which he has had ample opportunity to try out in little mission chapels before preaching it in the big church. He gets a glorious idea of his own wisdom, when the fact is that he may have been chosen bishop because he was regarded as safely and harmlessly conservative. He does not know that some irreverent folk consider him colorless. He does not realize how he has changed since he became a bishop: how the problems of the church and its meagre resources have discouraged him and at last he has relapsed into an easy indifference and does nothing; or, how, perhaps, the responsibilities and the dignity of his office have swelled

his head and he has become dictatorial and autocratic. He never hears what the clergy or the laity
think about him.

And the clergy do not know what he thinks
about them. There are very few bishops, archdeacons, presiding elders or rural deans who are so
cruel as to tell all that they do think. Had they
the courage and at the same time the grace to
speak out frankly, though considerately and with
due kindness, some of the clergy might learn that
many of their troubles begin on their own door-
steps. If there is anything unpalatable in what
follows, let the clerical reader remember that it is
written to help, not merely to condemn.

Why do the clergy find it necessary to move so
often? They will say that small salaries pinch them
sò desperately that they cannot be blamed if they
grow discouraged. But—they do not always move
to parishes that can give them more. And it is a
fact, which those "higher up" observe, that congregations often gladly and of their own accord vote
an increase of salary when the pastor is found specially deserving such appreciation. May not the
real cause be found in the fact that the ministry
offers desperate chances of slumping down into a
lazy, inactive life? In business there is always
some one to "jack up" a man; the minister is his
own overseer. There is no one to keep a record of
his pastoral calls, no one to note whether he does

an eight-hour-a-day job, no one except his bishop
—who, good, kind man that he is, doesn't always
want to complain—to know that he does not answer letters, that he does not keep accurate parish
record books, that he fails to make reports, and,
worse yet, fails to read suggestions. There is no
one but the choirmaster who knows how little
thought he gives to the arrangement of services—
and even the choirmaster does not always realize
that this is why the services fail to make a definite
impression. No one knows whether he has done
any honest work on his sermons, though the congregation may frequently make a close guess as to
the diligence of his thought and study. The temptation to indolence—bodily, mental, and spiritual
—is always there, and not always courageously
fought. Often the man gets what he is worth. Not
always, nor in the majority of cases, but often.

The minister wonders why he does not attract
better congregations. Would that he had married
a wife who could and would tell him that his sermons are rambling discourses; that he never takes
one idea, develops it carefully—and stops. Would
that he could realize how often he skips about, or
maunders on, leaving the congregation with nothing definite; perhaps only with a vague notion
that the parson has been reading a new book and
has not yet learned that nobody should talk about
a book until he has at least read it through. Of

course it is apparent, to others, if not to himself, when he preaches on the problems of the day without special knowledge, or on modern doubts and difficulties, only to show that he has not made honest effort to understand the view-point of the layman, or done enough hard thinking to prove that he really knows what he believes, and why. We hear much of the failure of the clergy to present religion in terms of to-day. The failure is usually attributed to theological narrowness. Actually, is it not the result of intellectual sloth, and the consequent failure to understand, or sympathize with, the difficulties of faith for men who know the new universe and the modern world?

Again, the minister wonders that the congregation does so little work; perhaps he complains now and then of the lack of co-operation. But he does not realize his own lack of administrative effort, or his maddening inability to do things in a businesslike way. He does not plan his own work, and he is hopelessly inefficient in planning work for others. He has no new ideas as to organization. He has no ability to inspire others to effort. He does not even display ordinary sound judgment in choosing his workers. He expects to get church-school teachers by casually suggesting from the pulpit that there are vacancies. When people offer their services in parish work he has not the faintest idea how to use them. Imagine a young girl, just graduated from college, offering herself for some useful service—and the best he can do is to suggest her arranging the flowers on the altar.

He complains that the congregation does not give him the respect due to his office, while unaware that the hard-working business man next door regards him as a diddling and doddering old woman, pottering around the house instead of hustling out to work. I knew one young minister who made a tremendous success in his first parish in a simple way. He lived in a suburban town and most of the men in his congregation took an early train for the city. He was always up early himself, out on the street, down at the station, and between 7.35 and 8.42 had a word with almost all of his male parishioners. It gave him a reputation for alertness; in a few months everybody knew he was "on the job."

Worst of all, the minister—and especially the young minister—suffers from a "priestly complex." Ordination is supposed to endow one with autocratic authority. He expects to have his every word accepted as law. He goes to a new parish and acts as if history began when he arrived. He gives the impression of being an "I, I, I man." He resents disagreement with his words, whether in "teaching" or "ruling." He has a profound contempt for diplomacy. (Of course there are "Yes men" whose diplomatic efforts lead to spinelessness.)

Nowhere is this lack of tact more apparent than with some of the younger ministers who preach the "social gospel." Socialists of every stripe among lay protagonists have an aggravating tendency to begin their addresses by thoroughly antagonizing their audiences. They are hot-headed in denunciation. They make no effort to present their appeal with charity and winsomeness. And some of the worst offenders are clergymen who seem to have a fatal facility for preaching even the truth with needlessly offensive aggressiveness. They are so fearful of sounding a cooing note that they never utter a wooing one.

Tact! In smaller matters, how easy it is to offend! I knew of one man who began an announcement: "It will be like a red rag to a bull for many of you; but hereafter we shall," etc., etc. A vestry came to one of our bishops not long ago to complain of their rector's lack of tact. He had noticed an inch of petticoat hanging below the skirt of the elderly president of the Ladies' Aid Society, and called her attention to it. "You don't regard such conduct as tactful, do you?" the vestrymen asked the bishop—and the latter replied that for a clergyman he considered it an astonishing evidence of rare diplomacy; the rector might have said: "Mrs. So and So, I did not know well-dressed women wore such things nowadays." Let it be said that the vestrymen did have sufficient sense of humor to depart a little shamefaced, though not yet strongly convinced of the general good sense of ministers.

"Priestly complex!" One clergyman whose complaints were vociferously voiced in a neighboring diocese closed his career with a sermon on the text which tells how Herod "gave not God the glory," and "was eaten of worms" and died. The lesson was plain: He himself was the Lord's anointed, and those who opposed him would presumably be smitten with disease and in all probability it would be fatal!

IV

Enough! Let it be understood that I am not wholly lacking in the tact which I look for in others, and that I have wisely refrained from singling out any of my own clergy in these examples of clerical failures. But I have made diligent inquiries elsewhere, have listened to the complaints of the laity, have heard in confidence many tales from other bishops, have had most interesting talks with a dear Methodist friend who is a presiding elder, know rather intimately a Methodist bishop and a Presbyterian moderator, have noted on the tablets of memory many things which occurred in my own circle of clerical acquaintances when I mingled with ministers in freer intercourse than they will permit now—and, even as I know the special temptations of the bishops in the way of megalocephalic delusion, so I know some of the faults of the clergy, which alienate their congregations, ruin their ministry, and account for their loss of prestige and their consequent discouragements. Indeed, their failures are due quite as much to petty faults such as are here catalogued, as to lack of vision to discern the possibilities of the Christian ministry in modern life.

But the laity! Ah, brethren, you have been waiting for this, have you not? Close study of the clergy reveals much that is unpleasant. How did they get that way? A close study of laymen may help us to answer the question.

Well, first, in the matter of salaries. It is often true that the average layman is pitifully small-minded about church support, with glorious exceptions in certain city churches, notably Presbyterian and Congregationalist. In spite of my defense, the fact is that it does not usually occur to the critical layman that he also is contributing to small-mindedness in the ministry by compelling his pastor to live a petty life, full of petty economies that cramp work and thought. He sees no injustice in paying his chauffeur more than he pays the minister, though not all chauffeurs are shining examples of faithfulness and efficiency. Nor does he understand that his attitude, and that of other men like him, may be keeping promising candidates out of the ministry. However anxious they may be to serve, their robust common sense makes them realize that they and their families must live decently. Allowing for all my admissions in confession and avoidance, there can be no denial of the seriousness of the minister's money problem.

What is there about Protestant Christianity, by the way, that makes so many church people small-minded in other things? Does the minister lack tact? Let heaven be his witness that there is no profession in which larger demands are made upon one's patience. We cannot imagine a leader in business listening to small complaints such as come to a clergyman from his fellow workers. If the head of a corporation had to deal with the rivalries of jealous women employees, he would go mad, unless he were empowered to fire as well as hire. The minister must not turn anybody out. He must smooth every wrinkle, or be turned out himself. The only other position in the world that offers a like opportunity for sainthood is held by his sexton, who must keep the church warm enough for Mrs. A and not too warm for Mrs. B. I remember one of my own parishes, where Mrs A came in one morning, shivering apprehensively, and then arose and opened the register; whereupon Mrs. B fanned herself violently and arose and closed it. They kept it up alternately, each comfortable until the other had her turn. Finally one of them was restrained by her husband. Was I lacking in tact when I told them afterward that the furnace fire had not been started that morning, and that open and closed registers had influenced their comfort only on Christian Science principles? Of course in speaking I remembered the Virginian's advice: "When you say that, smile!"

Amusing? Yes; but terribly trying, if that is the sort of thing one must deal with day after day. A clergyman comes to his work in love with the radiant personality of Jesus Christ, anxious to make others see the beauty and splendor of service offered to such a Leader. He starts to work and preach and pray, *con amore*. But he cannot keep it up forever if always enduring the pinpricks of captious criticism or the discouragements of stolid unresponsiveness. He suffers. Does any one suffer more than he, unless it be his wife? Of course she is rarely satisfactory to the women. She does too much, or she doesn't do enough. Like her husband, she has no infallible instinct which tells her that parishioners are ill, if they neglect to notify her husband or herself.

How can the clergyman keep his own spiritual fires burning when others have lapsed into lukewarmness? I remember, in my early days, preparing a sermon which I was all aflame to preach,

only to wait four consecutive Sundays for the
congregation to get over the evil effects of leaving
God alone during summer time; then finding that
the flame had cooled; at last preaching as pious
platitude what might have been a real message.

What is the minister to do if he finds few of his
people willing to inconvenience themselves in order to give regular and faithful service in church
organizations? What is he to do when, in spite of
real effort, the church is half empty? What shall
he say if it is almost impossible to get congregational worship, and he tries in vain to make the
people sing or take part in the responses of the
service?

> "Do you have music in your church?"
> I asked the country squire.
> "Oh, no," the old man quick replied,
> "Just singin' by the choir."

What is the minister to do if he cannot, in good
conscience, become a "live-wire preacher," a "go-
getter," or any of the other things in the way of
good mixing—which some of his men, it is true,
do consider the marks of an effective ministry—
and yet cannot make his people see the value of
religious habits? Most of our actions are habitual.
If we always had to stop, think, and reason out
our next move, we should never get anything
done. Our lives, in large measure, are regulated

by habit and directed by instinct. How can the clergyman who knows all this make his people see clearly that this points to the value of public worship? "The church is for religion what a social order is for civilization; it is an environment." The minister knows this, but he is bound to be discouraged if his golf-playing vestryman or trustee does not know it and complains when the church is not filled, though doing little himself to help crowd it. After all, a few really converted laymen might, conceivably, convert even bishops and clergy.

V

We discover many evidences that our laymen are not converted and that this is the real reason for the church's loss of prestige. Religion does not always play a large part in their lives. It is not that they have "views," they do not think much on the subject in any fashion. The conscientious clergyman often finds them all too ready to compromise with the world. Possibly he has convictions about marriage, for example, and they object to his offending influential parishioners who have lax views and cannot be made to understand that what is legal may not be Christian. Difficult Christian standards may not be accepted by a majority of his people, and they are impatient if he seems uncompromising. If he has decided views on

modern business, or preaches on certain national
problems or international duties, or expresses
doubts as to the permanency of the present world
order, he is regarded as a hopelessly idealistic doc-
trinaire, whose words are weighted with dynamite
—as perhaps they are.

There *are* men in the priesthood who are anxious to lead, who wish the church vitally and efficiently to minister to the needs of humanity. They
feel sure they could win to the church's work
many who are now outside, unattached followers
of Christ who are doing his work and yet have
not the stimulus of fellowship in his society, men
of strong religious feelings and convictions whose
absence from our ranks is their loss as well as ours.
What is the minister to do when he discovers that
he cannot win these men because they are bored
by the people who already make up his congregation? For undoubtedly many people do stay out
because of the character of those who are in. They
have an uncomfortable realization that church
people have little more than a code of conventional respectability, its outlook narrow, its temper puritanical, its orthodoxy sectarian, its morality prim and prissy. The truth is that the churches
are full of people whose religion is static.

What is the minister to do, then, if he begins
in a spirit of heroic adventure and later discovers
that for most of his people this spirit has been lost

through the stolid and stupid misinterpretation of commonplace men? What is he to do, if he finds that all his congregation expects of him is that he shall go on teaching them to meet life in a spirit of celestial resignation, submitting to every duty with exemplary forbearance and meeting the little inconveniences of life with patient piety—for this is all that many of them expect or desire in sermons, and even this they are apt to consider excellent spiritual advice for others, while actually rejecting it when they come to wrestle with their own problems. What is the minister to do who tries to quicken his church into life and learns that most of his people are not anxious to scale heights, do not wish to be set on fire with a quest for adventure, or reality, or joy, are satisfied to enroll as fellow Christians and church members anybody who has not been guilty of scandalous disregard of the social code? Is it any wonder that his sermons lose vitality when he finds everybody satisfied with a religion that makes no demands, sets no challenge, requires no resoluteness of will, no perseverance of discipline, no determined purpose, no largeness of sympathy and understanding?

Sometimes I catch the gleam of a new faith which the younger generation may bring to the churches. Many of us think they are "hard-boiled," whereas, perhaps, they are only anxious to appear

so, in their revolt against what they consider
"hokum" in all social institutions, the church included. Youth has no enthusiasm for the church
as an aseptic sanatorium where the ills of life are
to be healed. It has no enthusiasm for a religion
concerned largely with the salvation of meagre little individual souls. This present age is like youth
—wayward and conceited, but lovable; perhaps,
in time, it may turn to religion as a social force.
Without hopelessly antagonizing youth by attributing to it an idealism not always in evidence,
may we not offer a religion definite and challeng-
ing? We have been attempting, in a feeble fashion, to bring about a new world-order without the
inspiration, motive force, and driving power of
faith. It cannot be done. We have been trying to
base our morals on something else than faith.
That cannot be done. Except as a preliminary to
life with God, ethics are meaningless. The real
reason for decent living is that in obedience to
moral standards we liberate our possibilities of
spiritual life. Therefore, without religion as a basis
our ethical system has no necessary sanction. I
don't know that we shall make youth see this, for
a long time, but I am unwilling to give up trying
to make it clear.

Nor do I know how many of the clergy have
thought this out, but, despite the weakness of some
of the brethren, I know that many are beginning

to think about it and are anxious to teach it. How many of the older laity have the faintest idea of the problems involved? Is it any wonder, then, that there are weaker men in the ministry who feel that they are beating their heads against a stone wall and give up despairingly? What are they to do if they sympathize with youth more than the younger generation has ever guessed, know that the spirit of freedom, with all its confidence and hope, can meet its true Leader only in Jesus Christ, and yet find in their congregations parents who desire for their children only social success, are even less unwilling than are their sons and daughters to risk unpopularity, are themselves slaves of the Goddess of Folly and deliberately blind themselves to facts about which they are too timid to pass judgment? With all its faults, the new generation is intolerant of weak compromise. Perhaps its chief criticism of the church and of social institutions is that we find in them too much of compromise.

Yes, we clergy are a tiresome lot. We are often dull. We have little training in high-power salesmanship. We have small administrative gifts. We are no better, as orators, than the average lawyer or politician. We are cramped by poverty. We lack social graces. We too are not overbrave in our defiances; we feebly compromise. Many of us lose the first fire of faith. Some of us fall by the wayside.

But who is to blame? After all, the only material out of which to make a clergyman is lay material. And look at the laity! Will some one tell us how to make them different? Will some one from the ranks of youth, if not too angry at the slightest hint that he cares for idealism, give us a clear criticism—not simply a smashing and destructive bombardment, but constructive ideas as to what he wants and how he thinks he can get it?

MARRIAGE: TEMPORARY OR PERMANENT?

MARRIAGE: TEMPORARY OR
PERMANENT?

AMERICA is rapidly becoming a land of Mormons. The law forbids continuous polygamy, but we are substituting for it consecutive polygamy. To draft a figure of speech from days of horse-drawn vehicles, we do not drive in matrimonial pairs, but driving tandem is an increasingly popular custom.

For the most part, the Christian churches of America have been doing very little until recently to stem the tide of divorce which has made this country a disgrace to civilization. With the exception of the Roman Catholic and the Episcopal Churches, remarriage of the divorced has too often and too easily received the blessing of the church as well as the sanction of society. But at last the leaders of organized Christianity have begun a movement to check the evil, and many religious denominations and other associations have banded together to secure a uniform federal law bringing into line those States which are lax in their marriage laws, while allowing individual commonwealths to raise the bars against divorce still higher than the national standard, if they so desire. Personally, I doubt the wisdom of the plan. We have had quite enough centralization of power in federal authority, and experience must surely have taught, by this time, plain lessons in the futility of moral improvement by constitutional and statutory regulation.

In this movement for the correction of an evil scandalous in its proportions, it is not competent, of course, to lay emphasis wholly on the law of Christ. Christian morality is necessarily higher than State morality; its compelling power comes through voluntary acceptance of the higher law; it must not depend for obedience upon the power of civil authority. While faithful Christian teaching may do much to quicken the conscience of the nation, its authority and influence are necessarily limited when dealing with conditions which arise in a society for which the word of Christ is not "the last word." The State's appeal must be based upon the conception of marriage as a social institution, not simply as a church sacrament or ordinance.

It is the purpose of this chapter to show, briefly, the seriousness of the present situation and then to suggest that permanence in the marriage relation is the law of nature as well as the law of grace.

I

First, the seriousness of modern conditions in America. In spite of iteration and reiteration, the alarming increase in divorce has not yet been brought home to the conscience of the nation. It was not until 1876 that we had any authoritative information in regard to divorce in the United States. In that year the official reports of the Bureau of Census showed 122,121 divorces for the ten preceding years. Subsequent reports show an increase for each decade alarming in its rapidity. In 1886 the divorces for ten years were 206,595; the next decade showed 352,363, the next 593,362; the decade ending in 1916 showed 975,728—a total of over two and one-quarter millions of divorces in a half-century, with four and one-half millions divorced persons, and nearly 1,700,000 minor children left fatherless or motherless as a result of the law's laxity.

And the figures are still mounting tragically. The latest census report shows an increase of divorce in one year of more than eleven per cent over the previous year. In 1922 the proportion of divorces to population was 136 for every 100,000 of population, as against 112 six years before. There were two divorces for every fifteen marriages—the exact figures in 1922 being one divorce to every 7.6 marriages. The increase is indicated more clearly when we learn that just five times as many divorces in proportion to population were granted in 1922 as were granted half a century before.

The record in some States is nothing less than appalling. Nevada reached the lowest depths, granting 1,000 divorces—to many people, of course, having only temporary residence—as against 900 marriages. In 1922 this record of Nevada—ten divorces to nine marriages—had some close followers: Oregon, one to 2.6; Wyoming, one to 3.9; Montana, one to 4.3; Arizona, one to 4.7; Oklahoma, one to 4.8; Idaho, one to 4.9; Ohio, one to 5.2; Nebraska and Indiana, one to 5.4; Kansas, one to 5.7; Michigan, one to 5.8.

Lest it should be supposed that westward the course of divorce takes its way, we note that Texas has a record of one divorce in less than four marriages, Maine one in less than six, Florida one in less than seven, and Rhode Island one in less than eight. In the nation the record for 1922 was 165,139 divorces.

To permit the marriage relationship to assume such an experimental character involves results even more serious than the broken vow. Civil law has set up the machinery for unmarrying a wife from a husband and a husband from a wife; but that machinery cannot in fact be successful until it also succeeds in unfathering or unmothering the child who is the fruit of the union so dissolved. For the child to remain neither unfathered nor unmothered, after the husband has been unwifed and the wife unhusbanded, is indeed a glaring contempt

of court! Yet it is the sort of contempt the courts
have not succeeded in avoiding. After the arguments for divorce have all been presented, the
presence of one child effectively confutes them.
The child not only presupposes the family; it compels the family. It is the outward and visible sign
of an actual relationship between the father and
the mother. The State may conceivably repeal the
Christian marriage law; it cannot repeal the child.

From the point of view of social and legal complications, the diversity of State laws presents a
ghastly situation. Fifty-two causes for divorce are
listed, not counting those for which an annulment
of marriage may be secured. In twenty-seven States
there is no provision for a divorce *a mensa et thoro,*
that is, a legal separation without annulment of
the bond. Such a separation has always been recognized ecclesiastically as a lawful and sometimes
a necessary remedy for marriage difficulties, but
in these States such relief can be had only by a
divorce *a vinculo* with remarriage allowed, and indeed, to all intent, encouraged. One of the judges
of the Supreme Court of New York State recently
put the matter clearly when he said: "The finality of divorce is hideous. Separation holds the
possibility of reconciliation. Divorce precludes it."
In the same statement he protested against the
evils of alimony as a contributing cause in pro-
voking divorce proceedings: "Alimony represents

the sanction of divorce by the law and society; it places a premium on selfishness, slothfulness, idleness, and immorality."

The legal complications of divergent State laws add property confusion and personal entanglements to this social evil. Although, under the Federal Constitution, full faith and credit must be given in each State to the judicial proceedings of every other State, requirements concerning residence, legal notices, and other matters may differ in different States, with the result that often marriages are not legal in one place although so considered elsewhere, children have been adjudged illegitimate in one State though legitimate in another, a man or woman may be convicted of bigamy in a neighboring State after a divorce and remarriage across the border. Even the Supreme Court of the United States has not always been able to disentangle the complicated problems arising out of inheritance.

Of course, in so brief a discussion of the subject it is impossible to deal with many of the diversities of State laws through which these complications arise. An entire chapter would be needed, for example, merely to enumerate the varieties of legislation as to the age at which a valid marriage contract may be made. In six States a girl of twelve may marry, with the parents' consent; in one State she may do so without such consent. Small wonder that the author of *The Social Control of the Domestic Relations* should say: "It may reasonably be doubted whether any people in Occidental civilization has marriage laws so defective as ours. Almost every conceivable blunder has been committed." Other questions upon which legislators spend much labor are of little consequence compared with the vital question of the preservation of the home as the unit of our social life.

II

Conditions moral and legal have now reached such a pass that not only have churches and welfare organizations united in an effort to secure federal legislation and a uniform divorce law as a minimum of local permission to annul marriage, but the American Bar Association has joined in the demand. At best this regulation will but partially solve our problem; besides there are grave difficulties in the way of such federal legislation. Three things are needed, quite apart from any legislation. First, we need a clear statement of the law of Christ and a rallying of the Christian churches of America to a courageous determination not to countenance any departure from it. This will mean turning over to the civil officials all marriages contrary to Christ's law. Second, there will be necessary, even were a uniform divorce law secured, certain safeguards against hasty marriage; and, with this, faithful instruction by Christian pastors as to the seriousness of marriage, in the effort to check hasty alliances. Third, for those who do not accept the law of Christ as final, or for those who accept it as a spiritual ideal rather than a specific commandment, we need fuller consideration of the social value of permanency in the marriage bond as a prerequisite to any degree of domestic happiness or contentment.

The law of Christ is plain: "Whosover shall put away his wife, and marry another, committeth adultery against her: and if she herself shall put away her husband, and marry another, she committeth adultery." There can be but two questions as to the teaching.

Is it the *law* of Christian marriage or the *ideal* of Christian marriage? It is only on the assumption that Christ was not legislating, but was pleading for the highest and the best, that any Christian could possibly minimize the teaching. Certainly those who accept his teaching as having divine authority cannot possibly evade the issue, though others, who regard him only as a great teacher, may perhaps consent to the alteration of his precepts to meet new situations in a new age.

The other question deals with an apparent exception of allowance in the report of the words of Christ elsewhere, where the record is: "Every one that putteth away his wife, saving for the cause of fornication, maketh her an adulteress." It is the uncertainty of interpretation here which has led the Episcopal Church to allow, under very stringent conditions, remarriage of the innocent party in a divorce for adultery. Even that exception is further safeguarded by the provision that a clergyman may always decline to solemnize a marriage—a proviso which permits those to decline to officiate under the canon who believe that the exception is grammatically applicable only to "putting away" and cannot be applied to the remarriage. The Roman Catholic Church allows no exception; though, as a matter of fact, in its interpretation of what are known as "the Pauline injunctions" (covering the marriage of unbaptized persons) its actual practice is not beyond criticism. Recent instances of glaring freedom in annulment of marriages also lower the Roman ideal.

Other Christian churches have more lenient standards. There is not time or occasion here to explain them; suffice it to say that in many parts of the country the ministers are not much, if at all, in advance of the social and ethical standards of the community and are quite ready to marry any one whom the State permits them to join together —and even where some have scruples there are "marrying parsons" galore, if the contracting parties desire more than a civil ceremony.

We need, therefore, full and courageous presentation of the Christian ideal of marriage; nothing else can so effectively stay the tide of consecutive polygamy. The real reason for laxity of manners and morals is the failure of the churches to teach consistently and continuously the facts of Christianity and the morality of Christianity. The ignorance of multitudes as to the simplest outlines of Christian truth is amazing. Preaching has become "arid liberalism" for the cultured in the more educated sections and "acrid literalism" elsewhere. The result is that those inside many churches know little of the Christian story and less about Christ's moral demands, whereas others have been driven away from the church entirely; the latter, once they cease to live on the inherited religious precepts of a past generation, lapse into a modified paganism.

III

Christian teaching will but slowly reach the mass of the American people. Many of them, we have just said, are merely nominal Christians. Most of them would not hear the teaching, since they are not regular churchgoers. An increasingly large number of them are not disposed to accept the teaching of Christ as final. The present generation, at least, has so slight an attachment to organized Christianity that it will demand some-

thing more than the authority of the Christian
church before accepting so "hard" a law of life.
"What is the good of trying to keep two people
together," they ask, "if these people are wholly
unsuited to each other? Could anything be more
repulsive and repugnant to sound morality than
for those who have lost all the love that justifies
a marriage union to attempt to live together in
the marriage relation? Is it not better to dissolve
the union? And since to permit no remarriage
means the denial of another chance for a happy
life, why refuse them the opportunity of forming
another alliance?"

All this sounds plausible. Even those who wish
to be loyal to the ideal of marriage are tempted
to utter like sentiments in moments of sympathy
with the matrimonial misalliances of their own
friends. The special case is always a "special" case.
It is exceptional because it is a case near at hand.
It is on that account considered in a spirit of sentimental kindliness. The unfortunate domestic
disruption is a tragedy, and there is the disposi-
tion to view the whole matter leniently. Sympathy lets the heart run away with the head.

It is well, therefore, to insist that the marriage
ideal is based upon considerations which have
equal weight whether marriage be regarded as a
sacrament of religion or as a natural ordinance.
This is the special thought which needs to be ex-

pressed if we would really influence those who will not "hear the church."

The fact is that no marriage entered into with even the suggestion of a possible later separation has a fair chance for its life. Happy marriages do not spring into being at a stroke; they are made— made by slow steps and with much patient effort. A passionate emotional attachment will not so overcome the natural selfishness of two individuals as to make them at once considerate and forbearing and set them in the way of permanent happiness. In short, it is not true that some natural law of love can bring about a delightful situation through which a wilful, pleasure-loving woman and an equally indulgent, pleasure-loving young man will, simply because of their fascination for each other, immediately exhibit all the virtues necessary for the accommodation of differences of taste and clashing interests and desires, of selfishness set against selfishness.

There are marriages, of course, that proceed smoothly from romantic love to harmonious married affection, untroubled by any serious ripple of discord; but their success cannot be attributed to the supposed fact that mutual affection has made the way miraculously easy. It only looks easy because of the earnest purpose of both parties to make the marriage a happy one. A component part of romantic love is newness, strangeness, de-

lightfûl surprise; it embarks on voyages of discovery. From its very nature, therefore, romance
cannot last. It changes as it grows into something
permanent. We enjoy a new house because it is
new. Presently the new becomes familiar, and, for
those who are living happily in it, in place of
novelty come pleasant memories, comfort, satisfaction. The house is then much finer than a new
house; it is a home. In the same way a happy
marriage is one which passes from the transitory
delights of courtship and the honeymoon and becomes a permanent and satisfactory relation,
strong enough to weather the storms of life. Lives
fit together through bearing and forbearing; husband and wife make mutual concessions; they give
way in small things for the sake of the one great
thing. Two lives thus fitted together have tenderer
relations than any sentimental, romantic, or passionate pair of lovers ever yet found possible.

All this is somewhat platitudinous. But it paves
the way for the statement of a fact which, after
such considerations, seems self-evident; namely,
that this ideal of marriage can be realized only
when marriage is undertaken with no thought of
a possibility of its termination. Apart from the
repulsiveness of entering upon so intimate a relationship as a mere passing episode, the very suggestion of a possible termination through divorce,
with permission for a new trial, is fatal to the

first trial. Marriage begun under such terms could not really be tried. It would be condemned to death before ever the trial began. The first moment of boredom or irritation would be a step toward ending it.

Chesterton puts the argument so well that his words bear repeating: "In everything worth having there is a point of pain or tedium that must be passed, so that the pleasure may revive and endure. The success of the marriage comes after the failure of the honeymoon." Or again: "In everything on this earth that is worth doing, there is a stage when no one would do it, except for necessity or honor. It is then that the Institution upholds a man and helps him on to the firmer ground ahead. . . . That alone would justify the general human feeling of marriage as a fixed thing, dissolution of which is a fault, or at least an ignominy." And once more: "I have known many happy marriages, but never a compatible one. The whole aim of marriage is to fight through and survive the instant where incompatibility becomes unquestionable. If Americans can be divorced for 'incompatibility of temper,' I cannot conceive why they are not all divorced!"

Streeter puts the thought a little differently. He says: "The mystics say that a period of flatness and staleness, 'the dark night of the soul,' regularly follows the supreme experience of exaltation and illumination. It is often so with marriage. Enthusiasm and exaltation—at all levels of human experience—are inevitably followed by reaction. Love must be born again, and in a new shape, before marriage can realize its ideal. But many would never struggle through the time of blackness, if law and public opinion did not oblige them to go on. In marriage, as on the running-track, the fixity of the course makes easier the effort to find one's 'second wind.' "

To sum it all up: The real romance of marriage is that it is the great adventure, where two people think so much of each other that they bravely join their lives together and voyage in search of the Happy Isles, considering the promise of delight so great that they are willing to stake their all upon it. Take away the thought of finality and determination from the marriage vow, and at once its romance and beauty are gone, as well as its spirituality.

All this is true of marriage as a natural ordinance. Of course the case is strengthened when marriage becomes sacramental, as in the Roman Catholic and Episcopal Churches. We must remember, however, that when Jesus Christ enunciated his doctrine of the indissolubility of marriage he was speaking of marriage as it then was, and as of its nature it ought to be, and apart from any new revelation. The permanency of the marriage relation is not simply a matter of ecclesiastical order; the law is a law of human nature. The facts of life themselves show that if the institution of marriage is to result in happiness it must be entered into seriously, and with the deliberate intention of entering upon it as a lifelong relationship. Sentimental pleas for exceptional cases are made in forgetfulness of this fact. Stricter divorce laws are necessary, whether the marriage be of nature or of grace, if marriage is to build up a permanent structure. The hardships worked here and there by strict laws of divorce are nothing to the wholesale destruction of home life that would follow if easy divorce should continue and be generally encouraged.

There will, of course, be difficulties in any married life. They are to be expected; and they are to be met, not by permitting all who will to run away from them, but by insisting that all shall face them, and by facing overcome them. "One does not put away his mother or his children because of domestic difference; one assumes the relationship to be permanent, and adjusts himself to it as best he can; and in the vast majority of instances the necessity for adjustment promotes permanent affection. It is the same with husband and wife." So says Professor Peabody, and he adds: "The family thus becomes not a temporary resort for the satisfaction of passion, or a form of restraint from which on the least provocation one may escape, but a school of character where the capacity for ripened affection is trained and amplified by the sense of continuity and permanence."

This view is the only one that makes marriage possible for nine-tenths of the human race. If men and women are allowed to go about looking indefinitely for mates who are easy to live with, there will, in time, be a terrible decrease in permanent marriages. Very few people even remotely approach perfection. The wonderful thing, after all, is not that some marriages turn out badly, but that, men and women being what they are, so many turn out well. Where marriages are undertaken with the idea that they will be put through successfully (rather, that they *must* be put through successfully), a surprising number of happy homes are built up out of what seems to be most unpromising material. Failures there will always be—tragedies, marriages ending in conditions unendurable. In such cases divorce *a mensa et thoro* gives all needed relief. But to make tragedies of all the little serio-comic disturbances of married life by lax divorce laws—that is the greatest tragedy of all. Why bother to be considerate, why try to be unselfish, if it is easy to get away from the whole problem? Divorce is easy, goodness is not; why worry about being good if you can more easily be divorced?

IV

The sentiment of America—even its Christian sentiment—cannot be crystallized without continuous teaching as to the seriousness and solemnity of marriage as a permanency. The evil cannot be curbed, possibly, without legislation making marriage less impermanent. To protect children as well as parents from unhappy married life the facility for undoing the marriage must be checked. To prevent the impatient desire for separation, with a new attempt at a more successful union almost always in the background of thought, we need the teaching that marriage may not easily be annulled, and therefore ought not "by any to be entered into unadvisedly or lightly; but reverently, discreetly, advisedly, soberly, and in the fear of God." The present impermanency of marriage is resulting in hasty marriages by the thousands. Young men and women, after the briefest possible acquaintance, rush off to a parson or a justice of the peace and then on a week-end honeymoon. They come back, only to discover that they know little of each other and less of their often obtrusively present "in-laws"; that the problem of support is pressing if the girl is to give up a business position she held before the nine days' wonder of her "romance"; that if she does go back to her business office she becomes less and less a wife and seldom a mother; that neither she nor her husband has the slightest idea of marriage as a life of mutual concessions—the result being a brief period of bored regret and then a sudden convulsion that ends in separation. This description of marriage among the youth of one class of society may with a few strokes of the brush be changed into a like picture of matrimony among the industrial class, and with a very considerable splashing of color the picture may again be altered to depict the marriage of the idle, vacuous, or vicious rich.

The main sources of domestic instability are moral. As Doctor Peabody says: "Its chief provocations are not external, but internal; and its cure must begin with a finer social morality and a more worthy conception of the ends of human life. The problem of the family is but one aspect of the whole drift of social standards and ideals in modern life; and the loosening of the marriage tie is, from this point of view, a premonition of a general landslide of social morality."

What is the real difficulty with the present generation? We accomplish nothing by adopting a censorious attitude toward youth, always condemning and always complaining. Manners are bound to vary with varying social conventions; different times bring different behavior. But who shall say that the youth of to-day is less sound at the core than the youth of other days, when much was concealed under a superficial decorum, deference, courtesy, and conventional respect? The trouble lies no more with the young than with their elders. And the trouble with both is that we are morally drifting. Modern life seems to be without purpose or plan. Its chief characteristic is its aimlessness and amazing emptiness. Because we have forgotten some of the old values of life, and have lost our moral bearings, domestic life shares in the undisciplined, unsocialized, self-indulgent, wilful, and selfish spirit of the age. The only remedy is to make marriage so serious a thing that it will be seen to demand the generous instincts of mutual discipline, mutual forbearance, and the sharing of mutual burdens. To marry without thought of such adjustments of possible friction, with no intention to make sacrifices or to exercise discipline, is bound to result in disaster.

We need steady and persistent teaching, not in the spirit of complaint, but with the patience of true Christian sympathy and understanding, to correct the debasement of the popular mind which views the whole question of marriage with frivolous unconcern, a form of hilarious emotional experience which would seem to "recall the gayety of the grave-digger in a city swept by a pestilence." If, in order to make marriage a solemn undertaking, it must of necessity be permanent as a law

of nature as well as of grace, then we must strive
to improve the laws in the direction of that ideal,
even though sometimes the few must suffer for the
sake of the many. If the "complex agony of unhappy married life" becomes unbearable, separation without permission to remarry is allowed by
the strictest Christian moralist. If circumstances
make even separation impossible, "special cases of
social disease must not, according to the teaching
of Jesus, be permitted to menace the general social health." These are the words of one who is a
member of one of the Liberal Protestant churches,
not a Catholic. The language of Felix Adler, because he is arguing on grounds purely ethical and
social, is even stronger: "It is very hard sometimes to bear the burden of this law [of the permanency of marriage]. If I were a praying parson, I
should pray for sympathy not to become unfeeling
to the complex, secret agony herein involved. But
the law is inexorable."

COMPANIONATE MARRIAGE

COMPANIONATE MARRIAGE

I

THE latest proposal for controlling the glaring indiscretions of sex relationship is the "companionate marriage." It is only a new name for an old and ugly thing. Its chief advocate should be given full credit for the service he has rendered in an honest effort to give friendly counsel and assistance, and kindly human understanding and sympathy, in the problems arising out of the freedom between the sexes which characterizes youth and the present age. Even though we may differ with Judge Lindsey's conclusions, and feel that he is taking a short cut in a mistaken direction to reach a solution of the sex-question, we should allow for his honest intention of purpose. The situation calls for something other than loud denunciation. It calls for earnest effort in the reconsideration of the Christian position, and an honest attempt to deal with principles instead of summarily dismissing from consideration proposed civil adjustments. After all, the first challenge to the Christian should be to clear thinking as to his own convictions about marriage, his understanding of its purpose, and his interpretation of the church's duty in the improvement of present conditions.

Much discussion of divorce proceeds upon the assumption that marriage is the socially acceptable approach to sexual indulgence and that legal permissions for the contracting of new alliances somehow affect the moral character of the move by which one goes "off with the old and on with the new." But surely marriage, whatever its origins, never has been, and is not now, merely the legitimizing of the sex urge. Ideally, and more frequently in practice than the ultra-modernist supposes, it is conceived of as the union of two persons in a companionship which is the closest and most tender of all human relationships. Even in the marriage of mere physical attraction, there is more than sex urge. In the words of the English Prayer Book, the purpose of marriage is, not to "satisfy men's carnal lusts and appetites," but "the mutual society, help, and comfort that the one ought to have of the other, both in prosperity and adversity." It was, indeed, "ordained for the procreation of children"—a fact which is often forgotten when marriage is undertaken merely as a remedy for such "as have not the gift of continency"—but it is also a social sacrament designed to bring up such children "in the nurture and admonition of the Lord." The words are archaic, but none the less they are a very beautiful expression of the underlying meaning and purpose of the family life. Because marriage is a relationship ideally spiritual, it is not to be entered into "unadvisedly or lightly, but reverently, discreetly, advisedly, soberly, and in the fear of God."

Miss Rebecca West, in a recent discussion of the subject, declares that "liturgies simply restate in beautiful language what is already in the hearts of the participants"; that "few people present themselves to be married unless they are in a state of mind when they find it easy to promise to be faithful to each other until death, and find it difficult to believe that they could ever turn to other mates." The crux of the problem lies in the fact that this is precisely what is not the truth about modern marriage. While marriage is often the issue of romantic attachment, the ease of divorce as a remedy for unfortunate mistakes makes it possible, and even probable, that there is no such thought of permanency in many marriages. They are lightly entered upon, with the subconscious thought of the possibility of their being as lightly annulled.

And many other motives besides that of romantic love lie behind the conventional marriage of the day—motives of home instincts, of convenience, of comfort, ease, freedom from social restraints or social boredom, motives economic as well as social, motives of expediency—every possible motive, save that which grows out of the conception of family life as the sphere of mutual attachment, mutual helpfulness, education in self-subordination rather than in self-consideration and self-indulgence, with the discipline of adjustment and self-sacrifice, the sharing of problems and difficulties and burdens, the growth in unity and stability by the contagion of personality rather than the regulation of law.

Whatever its origin, this last has gradually become the real conception of marriage for those who have any religious idea of it whatever. Certainly it is the conception set forth by Jesus Christ. Only because the modern world has been content with much easier social standards and a far lower idea of the marriage relationship, are we facing our present distress. It is discouraging to find feminists showing small appreciation of marriage as anything more than the legalizing of sexual passion or a conventionally proper way of seeking individual "happiness." Even if the institution began as an attempt to regulate desire, it has (like other primitive institutions) grown into something better, with new sanctions.

"Companionate marriage" is simply surrender to the lower conception of sex-relationship. It throws into the discard all the lessons of past experience, and dismisses with a gesture of impatience the social code which has been built up out of an age-long effort to reach a sound organizing principle for social life. "Society," Doctor B. H.

Streeter reminds us, "consists of persons whose very existence depends upon the fact that there is a certain stability in the relations which they have with other persons." While granting that there may be, in morals as in science, free criticism of an existing hypothesis, he urges that in morals, even more than in science, experiment must be made on the basis of provisional acceptance of this hypothesis. A successful experiment is not likely to be made by one who does not recognize the value of that which the past has achieved, as well as its possible inadequacy. Doctor Streeter then gives this solemn warning: "In the sphere of conduct all experiment is costly; for conduct affects persons, and the consequence of action, upon the character of the doer and upon the welfare of the sufferer, are irrevocable and often disastrous. Whereas a broken test-tube does not matter, a broken life does."

A social code, therefore, is a necessity. Necessary, if for no other reason, because "the stronger must submit to restrictions which the weaker cannot do without." "The acceptance of a particular restriction is not a weak abnegation of personal liberty, it is a creative moral act which we recognize as socially constructive." The argument which Judge Lindsey presents works both ways. What he regards as a socially constructive proposal is actually a dangerously experimental removal of social safeguards.

II

One argument for "companionate marriage" is that it will solve the problem of the child as well as the problem of sex. Freedom of the sexes is now so general that it blazes out, all too often, in ghastly scandal. Why, then, we are asked, should the law be so severe as to compel those who desire the satisfaction of sex union to travel the road of illicit and concealed relationship? Sex union there is bound to be. Why not bring it out into the open, frankly acknowledge the danger for youth in seeking to repress it, make new laws which will give it statutory sanction, and give opportunity for new trials when experience has taught what experiment, and experiment only, ever can thoroughly teach?

The questions the Christian is bound to ask are these: Does the enactment of new laws necessarily affect the morals of an action? Does fornication become any the less fornication, if it be legalized? Is the situation really improved, because the law says that it may be recognized by the State? What does "companionate marriage" mean but that two people have declared that they desire sex relationship; that they do not mean to have children; that they wish society to recognize their relationship as proper and right; that they want to feel free to stop and take new partners if all does not go well; and that they are willing to pay as the price of social respectability and a legal status in the relationship, by declaring that if they make an unfortunate slip and have a child, it will be that much harder to reshuffle the cards and get a new deal?

That is not my idea of curing the present sex immorality. My firm conviction is that the only cure is education in what Christian marriage really is and the determination to set our faces against all that tends to break the sacredness of the tie; above all, education such as will show that sex wastefulness will mean the crushing of the moral life.

Moreover, in actual fact, are not childless marriages, especially marriages where there is the deliberate purpose not to have children, the ones which usually end in failure? Read the reports of divorce cases, and we discover that the problem of the child, tragic as it is, is not more tragic than the problems of childlessness. The childless marriage is an appallingly nonchalant affair. It is, in the long run, marriage that becomes a mere matter of processions—not merely "driving tandem," but a veritable succession of experiments, to the third or fourth readjustments.

It is difficult to see how such a condition can be improved by legalizing it in the interests of over-exuberant youth. By beginning earlier, with future trials possible, we are not likely to reach shining success in our social realignments. In plain words, we are simply travelling in the opposite direction on another pathway of moral "progress" which now obsesses America. You do not make it immoral to drink because the statutes make it illegal; nor do you make it moral to live with one woman after another, or one man after another, because the statutes make it legal. Morality is morality, and immorality is immorality, whatever the law may say in Denver or in Patagonia. The local moral mores may differ; but it is not the task of the Christian casuist to discover happy readjustments between his religious obligations and the customs or legislation of his locality; it is his task to teach the higher obligations, and at least to accept them as the standards to which he is responsible. Let America become pagan, if it will; but let us make clear the fact that if we *will* be pagan we do not help matters by passing laws which declare that we are in fact acting as good Christians.

Such is the protest the Christian may make. But a no less strenuous protest may be made from the standpoint of natural law and social morals. Let me quote Streeter again: "Marriage has survived because, along with a reasonable allowance to the claims of sex, it provides the richest possible satisfaction for the parental instinct. This instinct, so far as its *conscious realization* is concerned, is much less urgent than that of sex; but biologically it is deeply rooted, and it is much less spasmodic in its operation. Indeed, it is probable that for most people, though they are usually unaware of it, the psychological consequences of a life-long thwarting of this instinct (unless it is carefully sublimated) is a much greater degree of unhappiness than results from a (similarly unsublimated) thwarting of the sex instinct. It is the satisfaction of the parental instinct which makes worth while the loss of liberty entailed by marriage—which for the woman is very great, for the man far greater than feminist writers are usually willing to admit."

III

Because the Christian conception of marriage is higher, it is clear that the remedy for present evils must, for us, lie not so much in legislation—however useful that may be in curbing the exaggerated individualism of the age—as in patient education. Regulation there must be, of course. Doris Stevens has presented some of the arguments for general federal legislation as correcting the social and economic confusion of the present system, at which her "sense of orderliness rebels." The Christian parts company with her when she declares that "easy divorce is a civilized thing." It is not;

it is the reverse—a return to barbarism, with reservations. She herself admits that this civilized method "does not solve the very complex difficulties within marriage." The need of regulation as a matter of social safeguard, however, arises from the very opposite of what Miss Stevens conceives to be the conditions surrounding divorce. She thinks that "with very few exceptions, divorce is the road of last resort; it is the road taken after everything else has been tried and has failed." "People divorce each other only after a staggering total of strength has been given to the enterprise. Years of effort have preceded the break-up," she declares. "Various devices, depending upon the wits and energies of the parties concerned, have usually been exhausted before the ways part." It is her conviction that "people seek divorce with the utmost reluctance."

Personal observations are often unreliable. In this matter, however, statistics join with personal impressions in proving that divorce now frequently follows so close upon marriage as to furnish indubitable proof that effort to avoid the tragedy is only too feeble. The fact is, that divorce looms in thought as a ready release from the difficulties of readjustment, and the ease with which it may be obtained operates as an excuse for failure to attempt to make success out of what has begun to be a failure. Divorce, for the most part, results from the amazing aimlessness and emptiness of modern life. A pleasure-loving woman, with a taste for luxury and excitement, and an equally selfish man, married because of a sudden infatuation or because of social propinquity, soon find their romance rain-washed, the first bloom of mutual attraction blown off; and because separation is so easy, they never make any honest, earnest effort to translate the failure of their honeymoon into the success of married life. "Companionate marriage" is but a legalized encouragement of this aimless, easy-going, experimental attitude in the marital relationship. One of its most enthusiastic supporters has recently retracted his advocacy of it, on the ground that this result is sure to follow.

Here we reach the heart of the problem. Modern marriage does not often enough mean the "give and take" of companionship. Two men cannot live together without many mutual accommodations; much less can two women; never one man and one woman. With divorce ever at hand as a door of escape, trifles are magnified into tragedies. Not only is no "staggering toll of strength" used in the effort to make a happy marriage; actually, marriage is not even dimly perceived as demanding adjustments and accommodations. Divorce, to use a homely illustration, is simply an opportunity for the woman to pick up her dolls and leave; for the man to fly into a childish rage and likewise depart. If departure were a last desperate resort, if failure to make a success of marriage were still frowned upon, many more would somehow pass over the rough waters and find a peaceful harbor. With easy divorce, they actually do not give marriage a fair trial.

The only legal remedy for this weak solution of a social difficulty is a tightening of the marriage cords and the strengthening of marriage as a social contract. For even as such a civil contract, marriage (unlike other civil contracts) involves so much more than the happiness, or supposed happiness, of the parties to the partnership that it is absolutely necessary to make the breaking of the contract difficult rather than easy. Permanency in the marriage relationship is of its essence as a social obligation as well as of its religious character and sanction.

And this is especially true if we have in mind the children who may be (and, despite preventive effort, still are) the issue of the union. Ruth Hale (who still keeps her maiden name and has been freeing her very free mind in print) seems to have forgotten entirely their existence. Unlike Miss Stevens, whose orderly soul is disturbed by the confusion of varying State laws, she wants no federal legislation; she is quite content to endure the present chaos, until the new day dawns and marriage has become a continuous performance begun and ending as fancy lightens or fades. One wonders why any legal form at all? Why, but be-

cause there may be children? We are not quite
ready yet to leave them to co-operative caretakers,
though some have come perilously near it. And
even caretakers may desire open covenants openly
arrived at and legally enforceable! Miss West sees
this. She even appears to argue that the home
must be held together *merely* for the sake of the
children, though infidelity be blinked at, excused,
expected. Even "companionate marriage" must
take on something of permanency, if all precau-
tions fail and a child arrives upon the scene.

The three women who have lately discussed the
divorce problem seem to think, for the most part,
only of the woman's side of the marriage tragedy.
Miss West argues that unchastity is natural and
that marriage does not necessarily restrain it for
men. Her argument that divorce is to be discouraged because the marriage must be preserved for
the sake of the children attacks the problem from
an interesting point of view; but it does not seem
to occur to her to ask what is to be done with the
child, or how the family is to be held together, in
the case of the unchastity of the mother.

IV

We have recently had, from Doctor Björkman,
a full explanation and defense of the Swedish
law of marriage and divorce which is especially

pertinent to this discussion. It suggests a line of thought which may well occupy the attention of Christians and churchmen. The standards of the State can never be as high as the standards of religion. But may not the churches turn over to the State—insist upon so turning over to the civil authority—all such marriages as the State in its wisdom may allow as the best practically possible social standard for people in general, and give its blessing only to such marriages as are really Christian in spirit and purpose? That may, of course, be an iridescent dream in Christendom's present state of division, where refusal of the minister of one church to solemnize a marriage is apt to be followed by glad acceptance of the responsibility by ministers of other churches anxious to gain new adherents.

But would it not be better to rest content with smaller numbers and better quality? Is it too daring to ask the churches to be brave enough to demand real purpose of heart as a test of recognized discipleship? There would be some logic in making the plain declaration: If you regard marriage only as a civil contract, let the State make the contract and enforce or annul it. If you still desire a religious sanction to the marriage, you can secure it only when there is reason to believe that you purpose to undertake the union with real spiritual effort to "carry on," despite possible difficulties, in the spirit of its religious significance. The social chaos and moral disaster which would follow upon the conception of a purely contractual agreement might mean a readier return to the spiritual ideal. At any rate, the clergy would act as religious officers giving the church's blessing, not simply as authorized agents of the State.

For those who can no longer endure the agony of a union that has become impossible, there is always the partial relief of divorce without permission to remarry and this no longer necessarily means for the woman a life without comfort, protection, and support. Often it may mean a life in ruins, often a life of tragedy because of the utter loss of any hope of developing happiness. That is the side of the drama of marriage which few of us can contemplate without pity that reaches the point of agony. Yet the welfare of society sometimes demands the sacrifice of the individual. This is the law of social life in many other spheres, no less than in this. Has it not always been so? Will it ever be otherwise? Unless, indeed, with the strident advocates of individualism, in an age supposed to be socially minded, we insist upon being "happy" ourselves, whatever the social consequences for the community.

Yet I doubt whether the churches should give first emphasis to legislation—indeed, I am sure they should not. The remedy for social sin lies in

Christian teaching; or if the phrase be not allowed by modern radicals, at least in ethical teaching, of which we still believe we have the highest and best ideal in the social gospel of Jesus Christ. The real cause of the divorce peril lies not in loose legislation, but in the undisciplined, unsocialized, selfish wills of men and women, in their superficial view of the purpose of life, in the consequent failure to realize that the family, to quote Doctor Peabody, "is not designed to make life easier, but to make life better" and that it "rests upon the generous instincts of natural and self-forgetful love." The less the church has to do with prohibitive regulation, save in the way of emergency help, the better. Its real task is to lift high the ideal and to be patient in waiting for its slow acceptance through the regeneration of personalities. It must discourage hasty marriages and set its face against any sanction of such ill-advised unions by refusing to give its blessing to them. Still more must it discourage hasty divorces and sternly decline to sanction new marriages contrary to the plain teaching of its Master.

The objection may be raised that unless release from the marriage bond be made easier, marital infidelity will increase. The answer is that sin is still sin, whether it have legal sanction or not. The use of alcoholic beverages, *e. g.*, is not a sin, though the law has made it a misdemeanor. Successive sexual cohabitation the Christian does regard as sinful, even though the law may remove it from the category of crime. It does not become innocent because permitted to those who have gone through the formality of divorce; it merely ceases to be punishable under the law. Those who accept the Christian view of marriage regard with equal censure adultery and the legalized substitute for it which divorce permits.

The real need of the day is more careful teaching *before* marriage, more earnest effort to lessen the number of ill-considered unions, a more heroic attitude in declining to solemnize such unions, or to encourage their consideration even as a loophole of escape from scandal, rather than stern denunciation of the after-conditions of marriages which the churches have not had the courage to discountenance. Again, I come to the repetition of a phrase which is by this time fairly familiar: Not new statutes, but a new spirit; not legislation but teaching. We must train people to find out *before* marriage whether they are suited to each other. They must be given time and occasion for real comradeship. If the altered habits and conventions of this generation lead to such an acquaintance, free and not too much restricted, natural and easy, not artificial, we shall have counterbalancing values to set over against dangers we all deplore.

THE NEW HOME AND THE WOMAN

THE NEW HOME AND THE WOMAN

I

THE old-fashioned home is gone—gone forever. We may be very sad at its passing, we who owe all we are or hope to be to its quiet influence, but it is gone, nevertheless. The loss is a real tragedy. We feel that something very precious has gone out of life. Around it cluster so many tender associations, so many sweet and pleasant memories. The gentle and gracious goodness of the old-time home is something never to be forgotten.

Yet, with all its beauty and dignity, we would not exactly reproduce it, even if we could. It had its limitations and its weakness. Its outlook was too narrow; its interests too confined. It was a guarded "safety zone" in the busy highway of life. The business of its women was to make it a peaceful harbor from life's storms. Too often this meant that the woman herself knew little or nothing of life. Very seldom did the women of other days meet the troubled questionings which beset the women of to-day. Very few were their serious social problems. When such problems had to be faced, they were faced in the work world outside, and the men who met them came back to the home fireside for repose and refreshment only. They looked upon it as an oasis in the dry and dusty desert of life.

Just because it was a "safety zone," the home too often but poorly fitted those who were trained in its influence for the rough shocks of life. There were too many questions "taboo." Women themselves were supposed to be kept in the innocence of ignorance. When the children took their first flight from the home nest they left it not knowing the snares set for the righteous. When real life began for them, as real men and women, they were plunged into conditions very different from anything they had been prepared for, and in the new situation the sanctions and sanctities of former days had light hold upon them; the principles and practices of youth hardly seemed possible in the new environment. Their eyes were open to know good and evil, and they found their world turned upside down. The injunctions of the home lost their force; its teachings did not fit them for the unguessed mature tasks, and they did not know how to find new sanctions or evolve new principles or set up new standards. Thank God, there was a basis of love and truth and duty which kept many of them straight, but the road was strewn with tragic failures where domestic theory and world practice clashed and religion and morals broke to pieces in the downfall and overthrow.

Moreover, the home, with its carefully guarded life and its gentle women, knew little of the agonizing struggles of the less fortunate folk outside. Often, therefore, its religious faith and practice were conventional. More often yet, its morality was individualistic. At its core it was sometimes hopelessly selfish. It fostered a satisfied contentment which ought to have given place to divine discontent. Social questions were unknown; social responsibilities unrecognized; social obligations unmet. At times, like riches, its peace led to fatty degeneration of the moral nature.

It may be that I have dwelt too insistently upon the limitations of the old-time home. If so, it is because I take it for granted that we all know its beauties and its virtues so well that there is special need of pointing out its limitations and failures. At any rate it seems useless to spend much time in bemoaning the loss of old treasures; it is better to see what can be done with new possessions. The home of to-day, with the woman of to-day in care of it, may lack some of the old-time graces. Our sarcastic comparison of the family fireside and the steam radiator is one of those semi-humorous complaints which we make jokingly, knowing that the joke has a sting in its tail. Yet the new home may have something the old one lacked, and the new woman may give it helpfulness and force, even if for a space it lacks gentleness and grace. Indeed, the mellowing touch of time will soon soften its crudities. All new things look a bit glaring—even new homes and new women! And all new ideas are cantankerously rampant until the fact that they are first rarely denied, then widely accepted, and finally generally admitted as truisms robs them of their impertinent intrusiveness and forces their advocates into quiet and repose.

Actually, the modern woman is fitted—if she will—to make the home of to-day a real training-school for life. Perhaps she does not always recognize that as her task, and there is a terrible possibility that she may become a neurotic sensationalist; but the danger is no greater than that which beset the woman of other days, who was as likely to become a weak sentimentalist. However indignantly we may denounce certain departures from customs once accepted without questionings, we do well if we can cool our heated protests and examine new conditions and attitudes of mind with sympathetic effort at fuller understanding.

II

What *is* the modern woman at her best? She has grown out of healthy, athletic, frank, free girlhood into a maturity open-eyed and unafraid. She knows the facts of life. Social conditions are no

longer for her a sealed book. Men of an older generation may twist uncomfortably in their chairs
and blush to the tops of their bald heads when
they hear her frank discussions of modern problems, but at least we are learning that it is poor
policy to attempt to blind ourselves or her to the
facts. Our mothers ran to cover and closed their
eyes and ears to some things to which their daughters perhaps open their eyes and ears too wide.

Because she is open-eyed the woman of to-day
has found new view-points and is learning facts
with demoralizing swiftness. What wonder if she
cannot keep quiet and feels that she must talk of
her new thoughts? She knows. Being a woman,
she not only knows, but feels. And being a woman,
to know and to feel creates a very passion to
change. Sometimes in her enthusiasm she makes
the usual feminine error of assuming that new
laws on the statute books will correct all evils;
but, at any rate, there she is, bursting with knowledge and fired with zeal, and seeking an opportunity to give expression to her desire to make
things better.

This new knowledge has broadened woman's
whole outlook on life. That does not mean that
she no longer believes that woman's place is in the
home. Of course it is! But that is not her only
place. "Sex duties are only a part of woman's
work; all the rest of her is her portion in com-

mon with men, the priceless part of both of them which distinguishes them from the beasts of the field." Just as it is true that charity begins at home, but cannot end there, so it is true that woman's interests are normally domestic interests; but these are not her only interests.

All of which shows us what the feminist movement may do for the home. It will change it, of course. The new home, instead of being an aseptic asylum where the sins of life's larger activities are healed, may be a dynamic for service. As a social institution it will be interpreted in its fulness and developed and brought to its full fruition by the woman of to-day and to-morrow, because she will have accustomed herself to dealing with other problems, often essentially similar problems, in a larger way, and so will have developed her capacity for yielding a higher wisdom, exercising her peculiar insight and intuition, and transmitting her special influence.

To be sure, many of the new type of women have not yet recognized this as their real vocation. Here and there some neglect their children, or refuse to have children to neglect, that they may labor on a patient world without, instead of testing their talents on the world within. There have been particularly unlovely developments of the sex movement that have gone even further, giving us what Ferraro calls "the third sex." There are women who hate marriage and men, or demand the right to be independent of marriage through their work; there are feminists who reproach the women who marry because they have "betrayed the cause." There are other women who are either consumed by ambition or fanatically altruistic; still others nervously supersensitive or ascetically ethereal. We have all been brought to the verge of profanity or tears by such feminist types. They make us understand what Mr. Martin means by his assertion that man's moral duty to woman is like the relation of the rails to the railway train; he prevents her from destroying herself by jumping the track! After all, we discover that even husbands have their moral uses. If woman tames the man, man steadies the woman.

It does not seem too optimistic to hope that despite our fears the woman of the future will give to the making of the home her first and best effort. The joy of the new freedom need not, and after a time will not, dull the sense of obligation. Once the emancipation movement is well on its way, we may trust women not to lose sight of the purpose of emancipation, *viz.*, to make her fill her place better. We need to restrain our fear that she will desert the home. Rather she will learn, nay, is already learning, that education, freedom, organization, the suffrage—to name them in the order in which they have been won—are but tools to an end. That end is the largest acceptance of her responsibility and the richest fulfilment of her obligation—to make her house a real home; a home whose cultural life shall again radiate warmth and light for relatives and friends, as from the old hearth; a home where there are children and where the great task of woman is realized and accepted in the preparation of these children for citizenship and life.

There are, it is true, present tendencies which endanger the home, and for a time they have given ground for anxiety lest the emancipation of woman should destroy the home life rather than change its character. As Mrs. Snowden points out, such fears pay a poor compliment to the Divine Creator. The time will never come, she says, when women will cease to regard the home and children as their special concern. A God-implanted instinct has taught them this truth. "As the face of a flower turns naturally to the sun, so the heart of a woman turns toward a little child. The most rampant feminism would never accomplish the destruction of this natural and beautiful instinct, inherent in all women, toward life-giving and life-protecting."

III

The new home will be more efficiently managed. That hardly seems an overoptimistic prediction;

for, indeed, it is so already. Women now have time for outside interests because they are doing their inside work better and more quickly. This is, of course, partly due to the fact that so much of what used to be household work is now done for the home by outside agencies; but in equal measure it is due to the new type of woman who has the care of domestic affairs. Until recently the wife was quite often "a partner in an undertaking where her function was spending. She did not know a debit from a credit; she had to learn to make out a check correctly; she had no conscience about the fundamental need of living within an allowance." From now on she will become, more and more, a real partner who knows the responsibilities of partnership. Because many outside agencies do by wholesale so much that used to bulk large in the life of the household, the home of the future may have a better chance to fulfil its real function. Freed of drudgery and, in the case of the humbler home, of disease, noise, and dirt, its unique sphere will be found untouched and through specialization of functions made more distinctly its own.

A part of the efficiency of the new home will be the conservation of woman's life and strength. Here it is necessary to speak plainly. There will be smaller families, but better ones. "In the good old colonial days families of eight and ten and twelve were common, and the New England and Virginia churchyards are full of graves of babies and women worn out by motherhood before they had reached forty." This is not an argument for contraceptive birth-control; it does, however, suggest the wisdom of natural birth-control, and the woman's right to demand self-denial on the part of the man; the necessity, in fact, of common sense and reasonable restraint on the part of both. It is vital, of course, that the families of successful achievement should not die out; but exactly as economic forces eventually prove effective preventatives of an excessive birth-rate, so social forces may be trusted in the end to readjust present tendencies and perpetuate the families of the intelligent, educated class. France has been proving that a nation of small families is by no means decadent.

Again, there will be a conservation of women's health and nerves because the equality of relationships among men and women will eventually force upon the father his share of the common task of training the child. Heretofore it has not been a common responsibility. "Your husband admires the children," said a visitor to the mother of the household; "he is proud of them, but he seems to think they are *yours*." He had, in other words, shifted his share of a common task to his wife's shoulders; shunted upon her all responsibility

for the care and training of the children; had no
sense of real obligation save the duty to provide
for material needs. He was a sort of "animated
cash register."

The new equality will foster common responsibility and the assumption of joint duties. And the
woman herself will be a better partner in this joint
undertaking. In the past her children loved her,
but they did not always respect her intelligence.
As they grew older they ceased to care for her
opinions, defer to her judgments or credit her with
depth of discernment; they refused to be tied to
her apron strings. Well, the day of apron strings
is on its departure. The mother of to-morrow, with
her larger life, will become a real *person* in the
child's eyes. The fuller her individual life and the
broader her interests, the better it will be for the
children. They will look up to her as the equal of
the father; the father himself will respect her in-
tellect and step to her side to share a task difficult
and delicate enough to demand both of them for
its accomplishment. Intellectually the mother will
grow with her boy, and no longer will he "go out
from her influence in rebellious revolt, or submit
to her rule with a mind still in swaddling-clothes
until relentless life tears off the bands."

The old cultural method of the home insisted
upon absolute subordination as its first principle,
and self-denial as its second. The new will substi-

tute free companionship for subordination and self-control, and self-development for self-denial. The contrast may best be illustrated by quoting Keble's lines:

> "The trivial round, the common task,
> Will furnish all we ought to ask:
> Room to deny ourselves, a road
> To bring us daily nearer God."

As Doctor Dale once pointed out, excellent as the lines are in their way, they strike two false notes. They imply that the home is at best a substitute for a cloistered life, whereas it is immeasurably more, with opportunities for a more varied virtue and a richer and fuller perfection. The second false note is the one with which we are concerned here. Home, according to Keble, offers "room to deny ourselves." How petty it sounds, in the face of modern conceptions of religion. Without denying that there is truth in the thought, one may rebel against the tone of mind which gives it emphasis. God preserve us from homes full of such celestial resignation, where the first demand is that we shall submit with exemplary patience to every duty and meet with patient piety every inconvenience!

The home of the future, because it will be a home of more fully and freely developed personalities, will lose this false note. Not that it will lack self-denial—but it will be the self-denial of mutual forbearance and mutual sacrifice; it will have more of the element of give and take. Not simply husbands and wives, but parents and children will live on terms of larger equality; and this will make a tremendous difference in the training of children for life and its tasks. Subordination, of course, must still be a part of well-ordered existence; but subordination will have in it the element of self-control rather that self-effacement, of self-discipline rather than self-denial.

At any rate, whether this be too roseate a view for the present, surely even the most advanced of women will come to see that religion of some kind the home must have. The tendency has been to forget this, just as for a time in social work the tendency was to attempt it apart from Christian motives. In social service men are at last discovering that where Christ's spirit is not fully accepted there is no justice and righteousness wide enough or charitable enough to promise permanent and lasting peace. In the home we need to discover the same truth. Is it not barely possible that with all her enthusiasm for the development of her personality the woman of to-day has forgotten that the touch of the Divine Personality is the surest way to bring out the latent possibilities of the human?

Throughout this volume there have been repeated pleas for a return to the religion of Jesus

Christ; for a real effort to interpret his teaching in terms of modern life. We have summoned youth to find in Christ all the splendid things they now demand as rights; we have been pointing them to Christ as the goal toward which they must move, if they would begin the quest for real happiness. And we have summoned men to accept their part and function in the religious movements of the new age; to give Christianity its rightful place in the life of business, of commerce and industry, in politics, in national and international life. More men, and more from the ranks of youth, are seeking light than most of us realize. It has been disheartening, at times, to find that women (who in the Age of Innocence were regarded as the mainstays of religion) are often the last to respond to the summons for new efforts in new ways of service. It has been more than disheartening—it has been dismally depressing—to discover that their ideals often fall below those of husband or children. It has been tragic to know that among those of most alert and capable minds there has been a falling away from faith and an indifference to any spiritual mission—and this at a time when others are hearing the call to "rise up and follow."

If there are signs which indicate, among some women, such deadness and unresponsiveness, when those once supposed to be their inferiors in the realm of the spirit are now awakening, we have faith to believe that the balance will soon be restored. For, as Doctor Devine says, there is no sociological recipe for home happiness. Unless there is set up in the hearts of the children a reverence for holy things—and unless that reverence arises out of a recognition that these things are really held sacred by the parents—the home will go forever, and with the home the family, and with the family civilization, and with civilization woman herself.